THE
LANGUAGE
OF CONFESSION,
INTERROGATION,
AND DECEPTION

Empirical Linguistics Series

William A. Kretzschmar, Jr., Series Editor

Books in this series will bring serious attention to the study of empirical data (e.g., linguistic corpora, discourse analysis, dialectology, and sociolinguistics). Every volume will accept the actual utterances of real people as the basis for study. **Empirical Linguistics** fully embraces the "linguistics of speech," showcases applications of empirical methods, and includes textbooks that present the methods of empirical linguistics.

Also published in this series:

**Introduction to Quantitative Analysis of Linguistic Survey Data:
An Atlas By the Numbers**
by William A. Kretzschmar, Jr. and Edgar W. Schneider

THE LANGUAGE OF CONFESSION, INTERROGATION, AND DECEPTION

Roger W. Shuy

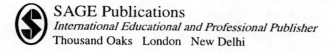

SAGE Publications
International Educational and Professional Publisher
Thousand Oaks London New Delhi

For information:

SAGE Publications, Inc.
2455 Teller Road
Thousand Oaks, California 91320
E-mail: order@sagepub.com

SAGE Publications Ltd.
6 Bonhill Street
London EC2A 4PU
United Kingdom

SAGE Publications India Pvt. Ltd.
M-32 Market
Greater Kailash I
New Delhi 110 048 India

Printed in the United States of America

Library of Congress Cataloging-in-Publication Data

Shuy, Roger W.
    The language of confession, interrogation, and deception / by Roger W. Shuy.
        p.   cm.—(Empirical linguistics)
    Includes bibliographical references and index.
    ISBN 0-7619-1346-7 (pbk.: acid-free paper).—ISBN 0-7619-1345-9
(cloth: acid-free paper)
        1. Police questioning—United States—Case studies. 2. Confession (Law)—United
States—Case studies. 3. Right to counsel—United States—Case studies.
I. Title. II. Series.
HV8073.S437 1998
363.25'4'0973—dc21   97-33752

            01   02   03   04   10   9   8   7   6   5   4   3

Acquiring Editor: Catherine Rossbach
Editorial Assistant: Kathleen Derby
Production Editor: Michele Lingre
Production Assistant: Denise Santoyo
Typesetter/Designer: Marion Warren
Cover Designer: Candice Harman

Contents

Series Editor's Introduction

The first book in the **Sage Empirical Linguistics Series** featured quantitative analysis, one of the possible avenues by which empirical analysis of language can be pursued. This book takes another path, qualitative analysis through case studies. While Roger Shuy does not count occurrences of linguistic features, he is no less interested in "the actual utterances of real people as the basis for study," the announced focus for the series.

And what case studies Shuy presents. They make for gripping reading. The facts of the legal cases are there, and the details of interrogation and confession. We learn that interrogations and confessions do not occur in two-minute segments—the impression that some readers may have gotten from popular television offerings—but instead as part of a process bound up with detective work and subject to every kind of social and legal pressure. Most of all, we learn that the interplay of language in interrogation and confession has its own drama that is every bit as intriguing as the drama of detection and trial. Shuy's detailed analysis of the discourse of interrogation and confession demonstrates that neither suspects nor law officers can afford to think that words mean just what they say. The condition of the speakers, whether they are asking or answering the questions, has much to do with the meanings of statements as those meanings are intended and inferred. The conditions under which statements are made also have much to do with their meaning.

We as readers can act the part of the proverbial fly on the wall, not for the events of hard-boiled detective fiction but now for the high stakes of real cases being decided on the basis of what people have actually said. And the verdicts are not always what disinterested analysis of the discourse suggests.

Forensic linguistics, here practiced by one of the founders of the field, is no less linguistic because it is also forensic, just as there is no less medicine in forensic medicine than in other medical specialties. Because the stakes are so high, there is all the more reason that linguists (and others) should apply every available method in the field to try to find the equity in confessions and interrogations. This Shuy does, whether by remarking on cultural differences in communication in the Panini case, or the sequence of question topics in the Jerue case, to name just two. From the welter of approaches in the different cases, general trends do emerge, both for linguists and for interrogators: linguistic analysis suggests practical consequences in law enforcement. Here is empirical linguistics at its best, not only in study of actual speech but in service to just treatment of actual speakers.

—William A. Kretzschmar, Jr.
University of Georgia

*To all those who have endured my fascination with this
subject during the past few years, especially my wife,
Jana Staton; my children, Tim, Joel, and Katie;
and my graduate students at Georgetown University.
All helped me hone and refine these thoughts.
To them all I am deeply grateful.*

Confession Event

The therapeutic effect of confession was drilled into me when I was a little boy. My mother attended an independent Bible church and made sure the basic tenets of Fundamentalist Christianity permeated my life. The theology of forgiveness required a preceding confession in the harsh reality of that world because unless we were forgiven, we faced a pretty dim prospect in the next life. The three-step process was to confess, be forgiven, and avoid punishment.

For the kinds of sins perpetrated by boys in the course of daily living, this process worked pretty well. I did something bad, confessed it to God in prayer, and felt a whole lot better about my chances of avoiding the eternal damnation of hell's fire. Whatever one may think of the theology, psychologically it was probably sound.

Somehow, my mother wasn't particularly concerned about my confessing my bad deeds to her personally. Maybe she didn't really want to know that her only son was capable of being bad. Maybe she thought that such actions would reflect poorly on her mothering skills. Because she didn't require this, I didn't share with her the dark secrets that I confessed to God. I let her think I was the perfect little gentleman that she expected, and we both avoided embarrassment that way.

The point here is that confessing one's sins to God is quite different from the act of confession that is useful in everyday interaction. One major difference is that when we commit evil acts against our fellow humans, we cannot expect to be forgiven easily or to have our slate wiped clean, with no retribution. I used to try to imagine the worst sin possible and how God would deal with someone who confessed it. Would God forgive a murderer, for example? Could a person who took the life of another ever expect to reach Heaven? Were the Ten Commandments examples of exceptions to the total forgiveness rule? Coveting another man's wife was of particular concern to me at that time—for hormonal reasons, of course.

These questions in my young mind were examples of the difference between confessing sins to God (with concomitant forgiveness) and confessing crimes to other humans (with concomitant expectations of punishment). A suspect who confesses a crime to law enforcement officers cannot reasonably expect to be forgiven and be sent home with the admonition never to do it again. Although the spiritual world may forgive such a crime, the social world will not dismiss it lightly.

A second major difference between confessing to God and confessing to other humans lies in the murky area of competence. We are much more forgiving of ill deeds committed by children or by people with mental disabilities than we are of people who are assumed to be mature and mentally competent, one reason why the insanity defense has risen to such prominence. The competence distinction did not obtain in the spiritual confession process introduced in my youth. I believed that my sins were no different from those of adults in God's eyes. If theology works at all, it works across the board. In fact, if someone had told me that God would take into consideration the fact that I was only 10 years old and forgive me because of my age rather than because of my confession, I probably wouldn't have made the effort at all. This, of course, would have been counterproductive to the whole religious enterprise because the church was intent on building into me a lifelong fear that would have been defused if I were to realize that, as a child, I would get a free ride.

A third major difference between religious confession and social confession is found in the different methods of encouraging and probing a person to confess. Religion—my religion, at least—assumed that all humans were innately evil and would, with uncomfortable regularity, commit sins. We were taught that even saints, like the disciple Peter and the apostle Paul, failed regularly. There was no need to urge us to confess our sins; God knew what they were anyway. Instead, we got regular reminders to tell God "all about it," in terms as general as this. Social confession does not assume that the persons receiving the confession know what the sin was. We have to tell in detail, and as a result, we often engage in a lengthy probing event to bring it all out.

Law enforcement agencies have additional problems in this area because many, if not most, persons from whom they try to elicit confessions are unwilling to reveal all they have done. The focus of this book is on the elicitation of confessions by the police and on how such confessions are interpreted. One might assume that a confession is a confession—nothing more, nothing less. But life is never that simple. Law enforcement is obliged to follow certain rules in obtaining a confession; otherwise, the event can be judged to be invalid. Because much of the language used in everyday interaction is less than precise, we can also predict that different listeners may understand words in different ways. The real world of police confessions, despite the training of interrogators, often yields confessions that do not signify what the police may think.

To a linguist steeped in the study of discourse, it seems odd that, in all the work on speech acts during the past decade or so, little mention is made of speech acts that transcend the artificial boundaries of a sentence. It is clear that complaining, for example, is a speech act in much the same way as warning or advising, yet because a complaint seems to require several sentences to produce felicitously (Shuy, 1988), it is ignored in the conventional speech act literature. Admitting and confessing fall victim to the same neglect even though the essential qualities of the more popularly treated, sentence-level speech acts are quite the same. Admitting, confessing, complaining, and undoubtedly others as well can be accomplished performatively or indirectly. Logical felicity conditions can be established. They do what speech act theorists since Searle (1969) have said speech acts do: They accomplish an act with words.

Perhaps their neglect stems from the analysts' inability or reluctance to suspend their sentence understanding long enough to perceive the appropriate discourse understanding. Thus, the following confession may seem to be nothing more than a series of asserted facts:

> Father, I have sinned. I lied to my mother about where I went last night. I drank far too much beer and got drunk. I sneaked into my house through a window so that my parents wouldn't hear me coming in the door.

On the surface, this text seems to be four sentences of reported facts. And indeed this is true. But the context of the words, signaled here only by the first word, *Father,* indicates that this is a confession before a priest. The speaker is admitting the bad things he has done. He is, in fact, confessing what he did, not just reporting it.

Speech acts can be popularly described as the way we use language to get things done. Some speech acts are of the pre-event type, such as making promises, advising, giving directives, warning, and requesting something.

Other speech acts are concurrent with their utterance, such as congratulating, thanking, or christening. Still other speech acts are of the post-event type, such as apologizing or confessing. Confessions look backward in time, a fact that, though obvious, brings with it certain constraints not realized by pre-event or simultaneous speech acts. For one thing, confessions require explicit and factual recall to the extent that pre-event and simultaneous speech acts do not.

A second distinguishing characteristic of the speech act of confession is that the confessor believes that what he or she did was wrong according to a recognized set of norms, that the confessor believes that the person to whom he or she is confessing also shares those norms, or that the person to whom the confession is given is in a position of authority over the confessor and that the confessor is aware that his or her confession correlates with some type of punishment.

A confession commits the confessor to the truth of what he or she says, whether or not it is ultimately determined to be true. As such, the speech act of confessing fits a category of speech acts called *commissives,* which commit the speaker to a certain course of action.

Confessing is usually associated with such areas as religion, law enforcement, prisoners of war, or therapy, what Sissela Bok (1983) refers to as *institutional confession.* Contrasting with institutional confessions are confessions that are more common to everyday existence: a child confessing to breaking a family rule, a gossip confessing minor infractions of behavior on the hope of eliciting even more dramatic ones from a conversation partner, a cook confessing to burning a roast, a teenager confessing to parents that the family car got scratched. Confessions report things that the confessor has done or thought and, as such, are a kind of narrative. They differ from standard narrative, however, in that confessions imply wrongdoing of some sort for which guilt and expiation are a desired end. For example, one does not confess to getting straight As on a report card or to being promoted to vice president, except perhaps facetiously.

Still another standard feature of confession is that it consists of what the speaker believes to be new information to the listener. It is infelicitous to confess what is already known, somewhat analogous to introducing the same topic over and over again in a conversation even after that topic has been resolved. Confessions, not having been previously disclosed, gain excitement and drama from this condition.

One form of religious confession in the Christian tradition is the testimony-time ritual often found in more evangelistic churches. Often, a midweek service consists largely of members retelling their past intimate sins, followed by expressions of release and joy that come by accepting the light of God into their lives. Many religious writers have followed this procedure, found in classics written by John Bunyan, Saint Augustine, and many less literary books currently available in religious bookstores. Such confessions can provide exciting reading, often both shocking and dramatic. But, as Bok (1983) points out, such revelations can also be quite manipulative in the sense that, by showing how evil we have been in the past, we are actually making a statement about how good we are right now. The midweek church testimony meeting well typifies such manipulation. Having grown up in this tradition, I can recall as a child how embarrassing it was to have not had a really dramatic, debauched life to have given up for God. Because my own testimony was never very interesting, I could gain little status among my peers for having traveled any distance in my past deviations from God's will. Ike Brody, in contrast, one of the church's deacons, could testify gloriously about having been the town drunk for many sin-infested years until God turned his life around. Now *that* was a powerful testimony.

Perhaps the best-known confession in American history is the young George Washington's apocryphal, candid admission to his father that he had indeed cut down his father's prized cherry tree. Every schoolchild hears that the elder Washington immediately forgave his son for confessing the deed so honestly. One parental moral commonly taught is that we should always tell the truth. But the concomitant and usually ignored part of this equation is that, by confessing all, we will receive instant and complete amnesty.

The popularity of this folk moral is not wasted by law enforcement interrogators. Although they are limited by laws and regulations about suggesting that legal punishment will be less severe if the suspect will only confess all, they are not blocked in offering what Ekman (1985) refers to as *psychological amnesty*:

> . . . by implying the suspect need not feel ashamed of, or even responsible for, committing the crime. An interrogator may sympathetically explain that he finds it very understandable, that he might have done it himself had he been in the same situation. (p. 53)

In most criminal cases, the traditional benefits come too late to be of any value to the confessors. Their crimes are so heinous that confessing them detracts little or not at all from the punishment that awaits. Unlike the young George Washington, forgiveness and amnesty cannot be expected for anything but remission of their tortured state of mind.

Just as there are two primary ways to lie—*concealing* and *falsifying* (Ekman 1985)—there are two parallel ways to confess—*revealing* and *self-aggrandizing*. Nor is the liar's common use of concealing foreign to confession. As with lying, concealment in confessing is preferred because it can be seen as less reprehensible. A common practice is to confess part of what was done, leaving out the most heinous or reprehensible acts that have been committed. Police interrogators of suspected criminals are quite familiar with such strategies, and their task is to build on these smaller admissions to get at the ultimate suspected crime. How they accomplish this is governed by regulations and laws to which they are bound, such as not promising leniency if the suspect will only confess and not threatening the suspect. The problem that law enforcement officers face in obtaining confessions is the subject of much of this book.

Some criminals confess to crimes, committed or not, as Ekman (1985) notes, "in order to be acknowledged and appreciated as having been clever enough to pull off a particular deceit" (p. 77). Such confessors are more concerned with their macho image and tough guy reputation than with the punishment that is bound to accrue. Criminologists claim that some people commit crimes more out of a perverted need to take great risks, to walk on the edge. The thrill of risk taking is well known in the psychology literature, and concealment of the risk just taken deprives the person of the recognition of this admired characteristic. Secretive crimes offer only a very narrow spectrum of potential admirers because crimes are, by definition, covert.

Because the confession event occurs primarily as part of a police interrogation, this book addresses confession as part of such interrogations. Equally salient to any understanding of a confession is the matter of truthfulness versus deception or lying. This book also addresses issues of deceptive language. The themes of interrogation strategies and veracity recur throughout the confession cases described here.

Considerable controversy seems to exist over what exactly a police interrogation is supposed to accomplish. One way to view the interrogation is to set it in the overall context of intelligence analysis. Harris (1976, p. 3) points out four major steps in the intelligence process:

1. Collecting
2. Evaluating what is collected
3. Analyzing for meaning
4. Reporting findings

The end product of intelligence analysis is an informed judgment. Harris (1976) defines it as "that activity whereby meaning, actual or suggested . . . is derived through organizing and systematically examining diverse information" (p. 30). He goes on to observe that the comparison of data is the critical step in analysis because, through such comparison, meaning is derived. The analyst makes a hypothesis, formulates a set of expectations, and compares actual observation with those expectations (p. 30). The analytical phase of intelligence analysis comes *after* the information has been largely collected. What characterizes effective intelligence analysis, however, is that *alternative* hypotheses are pursued, not just the hypothesis of the suspect's guilt. This pursuit is particularly crucial where only limited information is available, keeping in mind, as Harris notes, that "the business of intelligence is to probe allegations and suggestions of criminal activity rather than to build an evidentiary case" (p. 34).

The field of intelligence analysis, then, provides some important guidelines for conducting police interrogations and eliciting confessions. Andrews and Peterson (1990) provide a detailed description of these guidelines, many of which can be traced to the seminal work of Godfrey and Harris (1971), and as Marten (1990) points out, "[T]he intelligence process is no different from basic research: define the problem, collect the data, assess the data, collate and organize the data, analyze the data, and disseminate the data to the appropriate persons" (p. 3). Keeping these stages separate and clear is important because it is the interrogator's job to gather information in one task and to have it assessed carefully after it is accumulated. It is not the interrogator's job to analyze information while gathering it, although often hypotheses will suggest themselves at that time.

The police interrogation is but one of many types of human communication. People engage actively in different types of communication daily, such as conversations between friends or family and talk between buyers and sellers of goods and services. They also engage in more highly structured communication events, such as classroom interaction and doctor-patient communication, which come a bit closer to interrogation in structure.

One major difference between everyday conversation between friends and more structured talk events is that, in the latter, the status of the participants is unequal. The doctor, for example, has more status than the patient. The boss has more status than the employee. The teacher has more status than the student. With status comes power, and in conversation, power implies certain conversation rights. The powerful person can more readily introduce the topics, ask the questions, disagree, and give directives; the less powerful person cannot. The reason why this power asymmetry is significant is evident when one compares the *goal* of the interrogation with the language used to attain that goal.

Authorities on police interrogation differ somewhat in how interrogation is defined. Yeschke (1987) describes *interviewing* as "a dynamic human interaction having the purpose of collecting truthful data to be used for mature decision-making and just action-taking" (p. 25). He contrasts the interview with *interrogation,* however, defining the latter as "a face-to-face meeting with the distinct task of gaining an admission of confession in a real or apparent violation of law, policy, regulation or other restriction" (p. 25).

O'Hara and O'Hara (1988) also contrast interviewing with interrogating but make no mention of confession as the distinguishing characteristic (p. 94). The difference, according to O'Hara and O'Hara, is that interviews are conducted with persons "believed to possess knowledge that is of official interest to the investigator," whereas interrogations are given to persons "suspected of having committed an offense" (p. 94).

Aubry and Caputo (1980) agree with Yeschke that the purpose of an interrogation is to secure "an admission of guilt from an individual who has committed a crime," although they also point out that both the interview and the interrogation "are techniques for securing information" (p. 21).

Royal and Schutt (1976) agree that an interrogation has confession as its purpose, defining *interrogation* as "the formal and official examination of a person by the use of questioning and persuasion for the purpose of inducing him to reveal intentionally concealed information, usually self-incriminatory in nature" (p. 116).

From these authorities, we learn that the goal of interviews is to gather facts, the first stage in what Harris (1976) refers to as *intelligence analysis.* It is equally clear that these authorities differentiate interviews from interrogations, which have as their purpose securing a confession. It is equally clear that interrogations are conducted once it is reasonably certain that the person being questioned is guilty.

It is perplexing, however, how law enforcement could interrogate, following the above definition, without first interviewing. It would seem reasonable that the first contact with a suspect would be to bring out the necessary facts. It is quite possible that what may start out as an interview may turn into an interrogation once the suspect has produced inconsistent or conflicting statements, but it is not logical to conduct an interrogation before the necessary facts are revealed through an interview.

By analogy here, a problem faced by police interrogators is often trying to accomplish the entire legal process at one time, going for the home run when the task is primarily to gather information. Wrightsman and Kassin (1993) note, for example: "What is missing in most accounts of 'a confession' are the specifics—important specifics such as just what was admitted, how it was elicited, and why it was made" (p. 6). Such omissions are, of course, the result of an impatient or uninformed interrogation process. Other experts on the interrogation process have said essentially the same thing: "Interrogation is not simply a means of inducing an admission of guilt" (O'Hara & O'Hara, 1988, p. 111); "The real objective of interrogation is the exploration and resolution of issues, not necessarily the gaining of a written or oral confession" (Royal & Schutt, 1976, p. 25); "Avoid creating the impression of an investigator seeking a confession or conviction. It is far better to fulfill the role of one who is merely seeking the truth" (Inbau, Reid, & Buckley, 1986, p. 36).

Whatever the reasons suspects have for confessing, and whatever they choose to confess, the fact remains that the confession event is highly susceptible to interpretations that can cause considerable confusion, partly because most confessions are not made up of relatively clear and unambiguous performatives, such as:

I hereby do confess that on January 5, 1995, I robbed the bank on 48th Street.

Instead, confessions are often pieced together by means of an interrogation by law enforcement officers. Bits and pieces of the crime are elicited one by one in the form of questions and answers.

Because such confessions are dialogically constructed, they bear the imprint of not only the suspect but also the interrogator, and the end product must be analyzed in that light. Such dialogical construction leads inevitably to questions about what was actually confessed versus what was admitted, for example. A suspect, on the one hand, may admit to certain things that, in his or her mind at least, do not inculpate him or her in the suspected crime. The interrogator, on the other hand, may connect such admissions directly to that crime. And this is where the ultimate litigation will focus attention.

This book addresses the language used in confession events, both by suspects and by their interrogators. It is not a treatise on the law of confession. For this, one should refer to such sources as Nissman, Hagen, and Brooks (1985 with supplement updates), to Part 3 of Inbau et al. (1986), or to

Chapter 2 of Wrightsman and Kassin (1993). This book focuses primarily on the language of the interrogation and the confession, as well as evidence of deceitful language use.

Often, the major evidence against a suspect is gained through interrogation. Chapter 2, "Language of the Police Interrogation," describes three cases in which police interrogations were central to the trial. In each of these quite different cases, I was asked by defense attorneys to assist them by analyzing the language used. My analysis is presented in each instance.

Although constitutional rights are primarily a legal issue rather than a linguistic one, the law is incarnated only through language. The linguist's job is to determine how this is done, to analyze language for its potential meanings, its clarity or ambiguity, its cohesiveness and complexity. In Chapter 3, "Language and Constitutional Rights," I address these issues in DWI (driving while intoxicated) interrogations and in two criminal cases in which my analysis was used by the defense, illustrating significant problems with police interrogation.

Truthfulness is one of the four basic maxims of the cooperative principle in conversation (Grice, 1975), but linguistic analysis has limitations on being helpful in deception detection. But the systematic cataloguing of consistency in representing facts does fall within linguistic territory. In Chapter 4, "Language of Truthfulness and Deception," I report two criminal cases on which I catalogued inconsistent statements of witnesses for the defense.

Written confessions have great power to juries, who apparently find them more convincing and succinct than tape-recorded, oral confessions. Once a written confession is obtained, the case is often close to being resolved. But even written confessions can come back and bite the interrogator. Chapter 5, "Language of Written Confessions," describes my linguistic analysis in the case of a young man whose written confession was eventually thrown out by the prosecutor, who apparently recognized the interrogation flaws that my analysis revealed.

Some cases have what might be called "on-behalf-of" confessions, instances in which one person confesses, commonly, to a minor role in the crime and then implicates other persons by confessing for them. Chapter 6, "Language of the Implicational Confession," describes such a case, along with my linguistic analysis.

The police interrogator is sometimes tempted to take on the role of therapist during an investigation. Chapter 7, "Language of the Interrogator as Therapist," describes such a case and how interrogative suggestibility (Gudjonsson & Clark, 1986) was used by the law enforcement officer.

In my experience, it has been rare to have a case in which, though no tape-recorded or written confession was elicited, the police still claimed that the suspect had confessed. This is the ultimate challenge for a linguist who is accustomed to analyzing data. When I expressed this concern to the defense attorney in this case, he supplied me with depositions from which I could obtain patterns of language use that might well characterize the way the participants actually conversed in the crucial meetings that were not tape-recorded and for which only written reports were made after the fact. I was not particularly comfortable with this, but it was all the evidence there was. And the linguist learns to work with whatever data are available. I describe my analysis of this type of data in Chapter 8, "Inferred Confession."

Chapter 9, "Unvalidated Confession," deals with an alleged confession with even fewer data than those reported in Chapter 8. The Kevin Rogers case had no tape, no written statement, no stenographic record, and no notes taken by any of the law enforcement officers.

Lest the reader get the impression that all confessions and police interrogations are hopelessly flawed, I describe a successful and appropriate police interrogation in Chapter 10, "An Effective Interrogation and a Valid Confession." A suspect who was deeply involved in a murder case lies to the detectives over and over again in three interrogations. The detectives' style of questioning, their questioning sequences, and their conversational style all permit the suspect to self-generate her own guilt without even a hint of misleading questions or undue trickery. These interrogations were systematically and carefully videotaped in their entirety, which prevented the defense from making accusations of duress or ambiguity.

Chapter 11, "Some Basic Principles of Interrogation, Confession, and Deceptive Language," is a conclusion and summary. In it, I argue strongly that (a) law enforcement agencies permit suspects to self-generate their guilt through open-ended, conversational interviews, rather than through a series of direct question interrogations; (b) questions be unambiguous, clear, and explicit; (c) the interviews be information oriented, not persuasive trickery; and (d) law enforcement agencies make clear records of interrogations and confessions, preferably by videotape, but at least with audiotape, for their own protection, as well as in the interests of justice.

Language of the Police Interrogation

► Interrogating Versus Interviewing

In recent years, I have heard many law enforcement officers testify that they do not interrogate, that, rather, they interview subjects. From this, it is apparent that the image produced by the word *interrogation* is not one that some law enforcement officers appreciate. In fact, one such officer explained on the witness stand that *interrogation* conjures up browbeating and rubber hoses, practices not condoned by the police. However accurate this officer's assessment may be of the bad public image the word *interrogation* evinces, he was probably right to avoid using it. By using the more neutral term *interview*, law enforcement joins the large body of professions that carry out such activity, such as journalists, physicians, employers, social scientists of all types, and many others, none of whom would characterize their practice as "interrogation." The *interrogatory*, in contrast, is used without negative connotation in the practice of law, and the *interrogative pronoun* is a perfectly respectable grammatical category used by linguists.

If law enforcement is growing uncomfortable with the term *interrogation* and is replacing reference to the event with *interview*, it behooves us to consider the difference between an interrogation and an interview.

Interviewers make use of less of their power than do interrogators. An interview probes but does not cross-examine. It inquires but does not challenge. It suggests rather than demands. It uncovers rather than traps. It guides but does not dominate. It is "you" focused, not "I" focused. The interviewer's questioning sequence moves first from open-ended to *wh*- questions to probes with yes-no questions when appropriate. It completely avoids tag questions such as "You were there, weren't you?" The interviewer's probes ask the suspect to amplify or clarify but do not challenge. Good interviewers accomplish amplification probes with restatements, feedback markers (e.g., *uh-huh, yeah*), and sometimes even with long, silent pauses. It is astounding how people, when given a long pause, will simply keep on talking, realizing that the other person is not grabbing his or her turn of talk. Good interviewers accomplish clarification probes by paraphrasing or summarizing what the suspect has said and by nonthreatening but direct requests for clarification, such as, "I'm not sure I understand," or, "Could you explain that a bit more?"

In contrast, interrogators make ample use of their power. They challenge, warn, accuse, deny, and complain. They are more direct. They demand and they dominate. Open-ended questions are infrequent, and probe questions tend to be challenges that often indicate disbelief in what the suspect has said.

Although much has been written about how to conduct interviews in various fields and various subjects, little has been said about the general types of interviews into which each specific interview falls. For example, four such types are the information interview, elicitation interview, assessment interview, and persuasion interview (Donaghy, 1984, pp. 12-15).

The goal of the *information interview,* as is obvious from its title, is to find out things that are not known by the interviewer. In many cases, the best journalistic interview is an information interview. The reporter seeks new information, facts, opinions, and attitudes from the source. The information interview becomes skewed, however, if the interviewers begin with a clear sense of what they want to hear and influence or focus the responses only to the points they want to bring out. At such points, the interview becomes an elicitation, rather than an information interview.

The *elicitation interview* is common in some kinds of psychological or linguistic research. In such cases, the answer is known by the questioner even before the question is asked, and the point of the question is, not to uncover new content, but rather to observe how the subject responds. Linguists, for example, may research dialect differences and ask the subject what he or she calls a small body of water that runs through a farm. The subject is expected to answer "creek," but what is salient to the linguist is whether the word is pronounced "kreek" or "krik." The "krik" pronunciation is characteristic of Northern American dialects, whereas the "kreek" pronunciation is found commonly throughout the country. Likewise, psychological testing often asks questions with known answers, not to gain new information, but to obtain emotional, attitudinal, or other types of data. However appropriate the elicitation interview may be for certain academic purposes, it has serious problems for police interviewing or interrogation. Getting suspects to say what you want them to say, in the context of incrimination, comes very close to unfairness and can be seriously challenged by defense attorneys.

The *assessment interview* is common in the areas of employment, education, and psychology. Questions are asked, not to gain content information, but to determine whether a job candidate is appropriate for an available position or whether a student's knowledge or abilities are appropriate for grade or class placement. New information may come forth in such interviews, but not as their main purpose.

The *persuasion interview* is familiar to most people in subtler forms. Representatives of religious groups knock on our doors and ask us seemingly innocuous questions about our concerns for world peace and then launch into their answers to the questions. Likewise, certain market or political "surveys" give the appearance of objective neutrality but slant their questions in ways that have persuasion as their goal. Persuasion interviews are, in fact, not really interviews at all; they are hidden persuasion devices to get people to say or do things they might not otherwise care to say or do. Because they start out, at least, in an interview format, I include them here as an interview type.

The literature on techniques of the police interview is surprisingly slim. One of the most enlightening books is by Inbau et al., called *Criminal Interrogation and Confessions* (1986). These authors point out somewhat different strategies for cases in which the suspect's guilt is reasonably certain and for cases in which the suspect's guilt is uncertain.

The general advice to a police interrogator is to be patient, to make no promises, and to avoid letting the suspect make repeated denials of guilt, because the more a suspect tells a lie, the harder it is to get to the truth. Inbau et al. claim, in fact, that "a woman is much more reluctant than a man to confess a crime about which she has made repeated denials of guilt" (p. 117).

For suspects whose guilt is reasonably certain, Inbau et al. advise police interrogators to be confident, to accuse, to focus on reasons why the suspects did it, and to avoid the issue of whether or not they did it. Police are also urged to flatter lower-status suspects by referring to them as *Mr.* or *Mrs.* and to keep higher-status suspects subjugated by using their first names. The interrogator is encouraged to play the role of psychologist, calling attention to symptoms of guilt such as eye aversion, restlessness, or picking fingernails. Noting such behavior, the police officer is to point out that such actions are manifestations of lying. Anytime a suspect responds with words such as "as far as I know," the interrogator should view this as an admission and proceed accordingly.

Face saving is also recommended as a tactic to achieve confession. The interrogator is encouraged to suggest more benign motivations for the crime, such as the suspect's inebriation or self-defense. The interrogator should display sympathy and understanding, patting the suspect on the back and even condemning the victim with statements like, "Joe, no woman should be on the street alone at night looking as sexy as she did." The good cop-bad cop routine is described and encouraged, as is the tactic of playing one suspect against another to build mutual distrust, even indicating that other suspects have already confessed, whether they have or not.

For suspects whose guilt is uncertain, Inbau et al. (1986) suggest that they be asked about facts suggestive of guilt rather casually, not as though these facts are already known, giving the suspects every opportunity to lie. Such subjects should be given "When are you going to stop beating your wife?" questions, ones that presuppose that the wife has been beaten. Questions should intimidate a suspect into thinking the police already know facts they, indeed, do not. Tactics such as "Think very carefully before you answer the next question" and "Are you sure about that" are said to provoke truth from a guilty subject who fears that the truth is already known.

The above are by no means all the tactics suggested by Inbau et al., but these examples are adequate to show that the laws regarding police interrogation permit the police to lie, to flatter, to adduce, to ask questions roughly, to play act, to trick, and to cajole. It is equally clear that the police are not to promise or threaten or to pose as a fellow prisoner, an attorney, or someone else. In some instances, interpretation of the suspect's answers comes close to being dangerous. Failure to look the interrogator squarely in the eye is allegedly a clue to guilt despite the well-known fact that, in certain minority cultures, direct eye gaze is a sign of great disrespect. One wonders where justice has gone in cases when the police construct questions so that the suspect will not be able to deny guilt repeatedly when the suspect is, indeed, innocent. One wonders at the amateur psychology involved in the interrogator's interpretation of lying behavior. A suspect who says, "Not that I remember," may indeed not remember. Equally troublesome is the suggestion to ask the subject whether he or she had ever thought of committing the offense in question, with the concomitant suggestion that a yes answer is an indication of guilt. Inbau et al. also suggest that the suspects be asked whether they are willing to take a lie detector test. If they are innocent, they will say yes. If they say no, however, they should be told that lie detectors are not reliable, followed by a request for a truth serum test. This tactic comes close to threatening, if it does not reach it.

Of written confessions, Inbau et al.'s (1986) major bit of advice is as follows:

> In the preparation of the written confession no attempt should be made to improve the language used by the subject himself. It should represent his confession as he tells it, and unless it does, a judge or jury may be reluctant to believe that a defendant whose education may have ended at the third grade spoke the language of a college graduate. (p. 131)

These tactics in obtaining a confession grow out of specific laws about confessions. It is hard to believe that there was once a time when suspects were browbeaten and whipped into confessing their alleged crimes. It is harder yet to realize that such practices still exist in less enlightened parts of the world.

Within the constraints noted above, most police interrogations are conducted. Occasionally, however, the police stretch the dimensions a bit. Experts on law enforcement intelligence analysis claim that the end product of such analysis is an informed judgment. Intelligence analysts make use of information provided by investigations and make decisions concerning the implications of alleged criminal activity. Such analysis assumes that the basic information has been consistent and accurate. What to the investigator may appear to be good evidence of criminality may turn out to be inadequate from the intelligence analyst's perspective. Unless the evidence is explicit and noncontroversial, intelligence analysts, by definition, pose multiple hypotheses about the information they receive. One hypothesis, of course, is that the suspect is guilty. But efficient intelligence analysts cannot stop here. They must also pose hypotheses of innocence: How can the data be interpreted to support the suspect's claim of innocence? This is done both out of a sense of fairness or justice and out of the practical need to think through the possible defense argument even before it is made. When limited information is available, the formulation of alternative hypotheses is crucial. In fact, the role of the intelligence analyst is to probe allegations and suggestions of criminal activity, rather than to build an evidential case. For example, had intelligence analysts probed the allegations of criminal activity in the case of *United States v. John DeLorean,* they would have saved tremendous amounts of the taxpayers' money. The prosecution in this case gave every evidence of having only a single hypothesis—one of DeLorean's guilt. Had an intelligence analyst helped the prosecution form alternative hypotheses, the eventual acquittal in the trial might well have been anticipated. (For a detailed analysis of this case, see Shuy, 1993.)

In many criminal cases, the police interrogation provides much of the evidence against a suspect. Formally or informally, such evidence is reviewed by decision makers or district attorneys to determine whether it will be powerful enough to bring about a conviction. It is hoped, at least, that such analysis is also concerned with the administration of justice.

Following is an example of a criminal case that was based almost entirely on evidence derived from police interrogations. The example may compete with *United States v. John DeLorean* in its reliance on a single hypothesis amid far less than conclusive evidence of guilt.

► Case Study of the Interrogations of Steve Allen

When more than one interrogation takes place for the same suspected crime event, law enforcement officials seriously risk appearing, or actually being, inconsistent. It is generally believed that the suspect's inconsistency will trip him or her up and provide a wedge for the interrogators to get to what really happened. But inconsistency of police reports can also work for a suspect's benefit. Such was the case of Steve Allen, who returned to his Bartlesville, Oklahoma, home on the evening of June 11, 1990, and found his wife's body in a pool of blood on the kitchen floor. Exactly what happened that night is a matter of great dispute. After interrogating Allen several times, the police concluded that he was the primary suspect in his wife's death.

Steve Allen was an accountant with Phillips Petroleum in Bartlesville. His wife worked part-time at a local department store to supplement the income of their family of three boys. Allen had stopped by the department store at about 8:30 on the evening of June 11 and talked briefly with his wife. She told him she would be home at about 9:30 and asked him to drive to the local fast-food restaurant and buy a soft drink to enjoy after she got home. The two older boys were visiting their grandparents in Missouri, and Allen had their 2-year-old son with him in his car. He then drove to their church, where he was finishing some work in his role of church treasurer, and then drove home and found his wife on the floor.

As Allen explained to the various police officers who interrogated him that night, his car lights enabled him to catch a brief glimpse of someone on his patio as he turned into his driveway. This sight concerned him, so he left his 2-year-old alone in the car seat and ran into the house and found his wife.

Allen's first interrogation took place at his pastor's home at 12:25 a.m. on June 12. It was conducted by Detective Steve Gardella. Allen recounted what he knew pretty much as was indicated above. The police obtained permission to search his home and cars, and at 3 a.m. on the same night, Officers Mason and Potroff carried out a second interrogation. Meanwhile, the police had discovered a bloodstained, small tack hammer under some carpeting in Allen's attic. Blood stains on the pull-down attic stairway clearly led them to it. Allen had not mentioned anything about a hammer in the first interrogation, and the police now were suspicious. Curiously enough, Officers Mason and Potroff did not confront Allen with this information in the 3 a.m. interview. Allen brought it up himself, explaining that after he saw his wife's body, he was frustrated and panicked. When he saw the tack hammer on the kitchen counter, he picked it up and slammed it on the countertop and then realized he had blood all over himself from his efforts to revive his wife. Now the hammer had blood on it too, so in a panic he ran up to the attic and "threw it up there." At this point, the police accused Allen of the murder, which he continued to deny vociferously.

With no more to go on but this fragile piece of evidence, the police began to build their case against Allen. Several police officers were called to the scene after Allen had placed a 911 call for help. Each police officer made a statement about what Allen had said and how he had acted. The 911 operator indicated that Allen had not talked like a normal caller under such circumstances, evidencing a calmness and detachment that concerned her. From various police reports and depositions, it was determined that Allen's story about the dark figure he glimpsed on his patio was inconsistent. Further digging led the police to the fact that Allen had once had a brief affair with another woman, heightening their suspicion that Allen had committed the crime. Oddly enough, no investigation was made of any possible intruder that evening, leaving Allen as the lone suspect. It is a well-known belief in the investigation of murder that the person who finds the body is often the killer. Such a belief appears to have helped confirm the suspicion of the Bartlesville police in this case.

The evidence against Allen consisted of the following:

► The 911 call, in which Allen allegedly does not react in an emotionally appropriate way.
► The 12:25 a.m. interrogation of Allen at his pastor's home by Detective Gardella. It is impossible to know how long this interrogation lasted because Gardella's hidden microphone cut off abruptly at some point in their conversa-

tion. On the 25 minutes of tape, the first 13 minutes consist of talk among Gardella, the pastor, and the pastor's wife.

► A transcript of what is alleged to be part of the 3 a.m. interrogation of Allen by Detectives Mason and Potroff. Apparently, the police at one time had a tape recording, but the tape was lost before the defense could hear it.

► Police reports of several officers who were at the scene.

► Depositions of the same officers, as well as of other officers who did not write reports.

► Testimony of various neighbors of the Allens.

► The bloodstained tack hammer described earlier.

All evidence except the bloodstained hammer existed in the form of language and was, therefore, susceptible to linguistic analysis. The medical expert pointed out that the damage to Sandra Allen's head in no way matched the hammer and that, therefore, it was not the murder weapon. As for the language evidence, Allen's attorney, Alan Carlson, asked me to examine it for him.

The 911 Call Evidence: Allen's Odd Response

The government's transcript of the 911 call makes no mention of any distress that was clearly evident on the tape. Nor does it mention that the 911 operator insisted that Allen stay on the line during the almost 6-minute call while she contacted various emergency services. Although Allen does not scream or cry on the tape, he does display very heightened emotion through his intonation, his words, and his excited, heavy breathing that was clearly evident.

In her testimony, the telecommunications specialist who took the 911 call at the Bartlesville Police Department stated,

Considering the incidence, the circumstances, he [Allen] was very much in control. . . . The subject was very calm. Usually they will be so hysterical that they don't even realize that they maybe have not given me an address. They'll just scream that you send the police or whatever, ambulance, and hang up on you.

Later during the same testimony, the prosecutor asked the operator, "Could you describe your impression of Steve Allen's voice on the night of June 11th, 1990, Ma'am?" She responded, "Calm."

To counter the 911 operator's testimony that Allen did not speak with the appropriate hysteria, I called attention to all the places on the tape where his heavy breathing revealed excitement, if not panic, noting that these nonverbal clues appeared nowhere on the government's transcript. I also pointed out his following pleas for help:

- ► "Help me, please!"
- ► "Hurry!"
- ► "I need an ambulance!"
- ► "I need the police!"
- ► "Please hurry!"
- ► "I need an ambulance!"
- ► "There's blood all over the place!"

Each of these utterances was transcribed as though it had none of the rapid, high-pitched exclamatory tone that the tape contained. His demeanor was that of a very disturbed, upset man who was pleading for assistance. The 911 operator could not know, on the basis of this call, that Allen is a somewhat stolid, low-keyed, methodical individual who characteristically does what he is told to do in his work world of accounting, as well as in his personal life. He is not an exciting or excitable man. But to the 911 operator, he seemed different from the people she usually encountered in such situations. The prosecution team made a big point of this, possibly because they had little else on which to base their case.

Interview and Report Evidence of a Neighbor: Allen's Odd Response

One of Allen's neighbors, Bob Herring, seeing the police and ambulance arrive on the evening of June 11, walked over to the house and talked with Allen several times during the excitement. On June 14, Herring gave a statement to two local police officers. He claims to have tried to talk with Allen in the driveway of Allen's home between three and six times, each time asking Allen, "What's going on?" Herring reports that Allen didn't answer but, instead, paced "back and forth between the door and the driveway area, back and forth . . . his hands in his head [*sic*], something like this" (demonstrates). The interrogator then clarified for the record that Herring had demonstrated by sitting on the floor with his knees raised and his elbows resting on his knees and his head in his hands. Herring then opined that Allen was in shock, "but Steve doesn't say anything . . . does not talk to me. That bugs me a little bit, we're all in shock." Next, Herring reports, "he grabs my left arm with his right hand and says, 'Bob, call my pastor. His name is Bill Brum-something.' " Finally, the neighbor states, "They get into the car and I tap on the window and open the door and say, 'Steve, what's, how are you, what's going on,' and he just kinda dumbfound, he just sits there . . . maybe if I saw what he saw maybe I wouldn't talk to anybody, I don't know, but the fact that he said nothing to me strikes me as odd."

The prosecution made a great deal of Herring's observations, correlating them with the 911 operator's opinions of Allen's odd behavior. Curiously enough, however, Herring's observations that Allen was in shock, head in hands, and dumbfounded appeared to contradict the operator's opinion, as I pointed out in court. In an undated follow-up telephone transcript of a conversation with the police, Herring repeated his concern over the fact that Allen would not talk with him and added, "There was no hysteria of him walking in and finding his wife like this. . . . I couldn't have been that cool if I'd walked in and found my wife butchered." The dramatic difference between Herring's interview opinion and the follow-up telephone conversation (for which no tape was made available—also presumably lost) gives the impression of being some sort of rehabilitation to remind or at least soften Herring's earlier contradiction of the 911 operator's feelings about Allen's demeanor.

Testimony of Various Police Officers: The Intruder

The most important issue raised by the prosecution was that Allen was inconsistent in what he reported about the intruder he allegedly saw briefly on his patio as he turned in the driveway. The police clearly believed that Allen was making up his story as he went along, occasionally losing control of details. The prosecution called on this supposed inconsistency with details as evidence of Allen's guilt.

A rather straightforward comparative analysis suggested itself. I prepared a chart of all of Allen's tape-recorded references to the patio intruder with the memorialized statements made by all other people who interrogated Allen.

Such a procedure would yield three benefits. First, it would reveal whether Allen was consistent in his many discussions about the intruder during the hours following the murder. Second, it would be possible to check the accuracy of the investigator's representation of what Allen said with Allen's actual words on tape. Third, when multiple interrogators and multiple interrogations are involved, as in this case, it would be possible to compare the consistency of their different representations of the same event.

Allen's Tape-Recorded Words

In the three verifiable sources of information available—the 911 call tape, the 12:25 a.m. Gardella interrogation, and the 3:00 a.m. Mason-Potroff interrogation—Allen said the following about the intruder:

911 Call

▶ "I saw somebody running through my back yard."
▶ "I pulled in and they'd gone."
▶ "He saw me, turned and went to other direction."

12:25 Interrogation

▶ "My lights caught somebody on the patio."
▶ "I don't know what door he came out of."
▶ "He was on the patio."
▶ "He turned in the opposite direction."

3:00 a.m. Interrogation

▶ "I turned into the driveway and my lights panned."
▶ "I got a glimpse of someone."
▶ "They turned."
▶ "I had a sweeping glance."

In these three different statements, Allen gives the same information consistently.

It should be noted here that, at the start of the 911 call, Allen advised, "I saw somebody running through my back yard." The operator tells Allen to hold on, and she contacts a police officer and tells him, "He advised somebody had ran out the back door." Allen did not mention a back door. The operator then returns to Allen, asks for a description of the intruder, and then asks, "OK, he, he came out the back door, right?" Allen responds, "Yes, I have (inaudible) at my house." For some reason, the operator took Allen's response as an affirmation that he saw the intruder come out the back door. Even with the inaudible, static-blocked words in his sentence, it is clear that Allen was saying that he has a back door, not that he saw the person running out the door. Later, the operator calls another police officer and confirms her understanding of this: "Advised he went out the back door."

The operator developed a schema about the back door that was reified in her advice to the police, irrespective of what Allen actually said. This point became central in the prosecution's case against Allen despite its shaky origin.

Two officers who interrogated Allen—Detective Gardella and Officer Otte—report exactly what Allen said in his tape-recorded statements. The reports of the first two officers to arrive at the scene—Sergeant Davis and Patrolman Grayson—report something quite different. The two separate reports of these officers add that Allen said the intruder *came through* the back door and that the intruder *went through* that door. It is not contested that the audible voices of officers on the 911 tape, when the operator contacted their units, were those of Davis and Grayson. In her deposition, the 911 operator admitted to Defense Attorney Carlson that she had erroneously introduced the notion that Allen had reported that the intruder ran out the back door. Davis and Grayson clearly heard this and apparently believed that Allen said it.

If we had had a tape recording at the scene of the crime when first Grayson, then Davis, arrived at the house, we might have heard Grayson or Davis or both ask about the back door because it was fresh in their awareness from the 911 operator's error. If they had asked this at all, Allen may well have believed they were asking him to speculate on how the intruder entered or left or both. The intruder was obviously not foremost in his mind at that time; his wife's condition was. Davis and Grayson then may have taken this speculation as a personal observation by Allen. But the fact that it was not Allen's personal observation is supported by the following:

- ▶ Allen never says this on tape.
- ▶ Allen denies that he said this on tape in the 12:25 interrogation by Gardella: "I don't know what door he came out of."
- ▶ Officer Grayson's own confusion and inconsistency about other things that he observed, as evidenced by his deposition testimony:
  - ▶ "I later went into the area (living room) and I observed the door was *open* but the screen door was locked."
  - ▶ "I didn't check the screen door myself. I don't know of any other officers checking it because I was in the garage securing the scene."

> ► "No, I didn't ever go over and check the screen door myself to *see if it was locked.* My superior officer (Davis) was who I relied on to determine that the screen door was locked. He stated to me that the screen door's locked."

We learn from this that "to observe," at least to one police officer, means believing what someone else tells him—hardly acceptable practice for an officer of the law.

Having demonstrated that the notion that Allen was inconsistent in referring to the intruder was based on an erroneous assumption by the 911 operator and having pointed out the untrustworthiness of Officer Grayson's testimony, we are left with Sergeant Davis as the focal point on this matter. His strongest testimony about the intruder and the back door was couched in the passive voice:

> ► "*I was told* at one point the subject exited the family room through the door which I found to be locked."
> ► "*I get the story* that . . . he ran around the patio."

Davis never specifies who told him this but leaves the impression that it was Allen. Clues to Davis's reliability as a witness were also highlighted by his inconsistent representations about other matters. For example, when asked what Allen said about the intruder when he arrived on the scene, Davis gives the following contradictory description at different points in his testimony:

> ► "He went out that door."
> ► "He was standing on the corner of the house."
> ► "He was standing outside as Allen came up the driveway."
> ► "He was standing in the family room."
> ► "He stood there in the doorway."
> ► "He ran down the patio."
> ► "He ran around the corner."

Other police officers at the scene testified that Allen said the intruder ran. Davis is the only one to point out that he was "standing there," and this with no consistency.

Later, in his deposition testimony, the following exchange took place between defense attorney Carlson and Sergeant Davis:

Davis: After I said, "Did you see the suspect?" he said, "Yeah, but it was too fast. I couldn't describe him. He ran out that door." You can't change my assumption that I thought he saw the guy run out the door.

Carlson: But you agree with me that you assumed that he saw him run out that door. Is that your assumption?

Davis: Yes.

On the record, Defense Attorney Carlson had gotten Davis to admit that what he had testified to was, indeed, only Davis's assumption, and not an accurate record of what Allen had said.

Other Inconsistencies Between Reports and Testimony of the Police

The 911 operator's mistaken assumption about what Allen told her about the intruder running out the back door created a chain of further inferences as well. Officer Davis noted in his report that this same back door was locked from the inside. Building on the erroneous notion that Allen had said the intruder went out that door, Davis thought he had found an inconsistency when he checked the back door and found it locked from the inside. Or did he? On this topic, Davis offered the following inconsistent information in his deposition testimony:

▶ "I didn't even touch the door. I just reached around inside and backhanded the latch on the screen door to see if it was locked."

▶ "Well, I assumed it was locked when it wouldn't open."

We will never know exactly what Sergeant Davis meant by "backhanding" the latch, but it is clear that, once again, the sergeant's testimony was based on assumption. As was later revealed, the door in question was an unusually balky one, often proving difficult to open even for the Allen family.

Likewise, neighbor Bob Herring said repeatedly in his police interrogation that Allen would not talk to him. In his deposition with Defense Attorney Carlson, however, the following was said:

Carlson: Steve did communicate to you, didn't he, Mr. Herring, there at his residence? Matter of fact, he said, "Take care of Aaron."

Herring: Yes sir.

Even in his police interrogation, Herring reported that Allen had asked him to call his pastor. Now we know that Allen had said at least two things to his neighbor, rather than, as Herring put it, "He wouldn't say anything to me."

Two other police officers at the scene also filed reports with quite different descriptions of the same event. Officer Holland wrote: "The sheriff asked Allen if he could describe the suspect and he said he could not. The sheriff then asked the following question: 'That light-colored shirt the suspect has on, did it have any lettering?' Allen responded, 'No, it was just a light-colored shirt.' " In contrast, Officer Silver reported this as follows: "He said that his clothes were dark and plain-colored . . . and that the clothes had no markings on them that he could recall. . . . I asked him if he could tell me some more about the writing on his clothes or what he saw, maybe a logo on his clothing or writing may have said. And he answered he didn't recall."

Were the suspect's clothes light or dark? From Allen's tape-recorded interrogation, we get no clue to this. But during the excitement at the scene, with police, fire, and emergency personnel swarming around, each apparently getting a turn at Allen, a patchwork of inconsistency emerges in the officers' reports and memories. The police intelligence issue is whether such inconsistencies were produced by the sender of the messages or by the receivers.

Detective Mason, one of the officers who conducted the 3 a.m. interrogation, apparently had a memory lapse between the time of his tape-recorded interrogation and his deposition testimony. At 3 a.m., the interrogation transcript shows, Allen says of the intruder, "It was just a dark figure is all I remember." By the time of his deposition, Mason had forgotten that Allen had told him that he got only a brief glimpse of this person from the headlights of his car:

Carlson: Did he say why he couldn't describe him?
Mason: No, he did not.
Carlson: There's no reference to the fact that it's too dark?
Mason: No, Sir.

Mason's memory also failed him between the time he submitted his report of the interrogation and his deposition testimony:

Report: Det. Potroff and myself went over to Reverend Brummit's house . . . and visited with Steven Allen, which was the suspect in this thing at that time.

Compare this with Officer Mason's deposition testimony:

Carlson: Was he a suspect when you interviewed him?

Mason: No, Sir, not at that particular time, he wasn't. I say no. Everybody was a suspect at that time because we really didn't know where to go.

Ignoring, for a moment at least, the ludicrousness of everybody being a suspect (whatever that might mean), the stark inconsistency of Mason's statements about Allen being suspect stand out.

Likewise, in the government's own transcript of the 3 a.m. interrogation (remember, no tape was available because the police claim to have lost it), the topic of the bloody hammer is brought up by Allen. Yet, in his deposition testimony, Officer Mason claimed: "I brought up the subject that there was some blood drippings going up the stairway into the attic that Chief Holland had found. . . . I brought up the fact about the blood spots."

Sergeant Davis was equally inconsistent about whether a light was on in the family room when he arrived. His deposition testimony is as follows:

Carlson: So you're telling me that the light was on or off?

Davis: Off.

And later, in the same deposition:

Carlson: Now are you sure that the light in the family room was off?

Davis: I don't know.

By now, it should be clear that consistency is not particularly evident in the observations and memories of the many police who were at the scene, wrote up police reports, and offered testimony. Sergeant Davis and his underling, Officer Grayson, reported that Allen was sweating profusely. Neighbor Bob Herring reported that he didn't notice any sweat. Officer Silver testified first that he asked Allen what race the intruder was and then admitted he couldn't recall whether he had asked this question. Combine these rather minor issues with the major ones noted above, and one gets the distinct picture of a somewhat amateurish investigation by police officers who were quick to place the blame on the only available suspect.

The linguistic analysis employed here was *topic analysis*. Out of the hundreds of pages of transcripts of tapes and testimony and police reports, I charted every instance that occurred on the topic of the intruder. This process enabled me to discover inconsistencies between the primary data, which were tape recorded and therefore verifiable, with secondary data, which reflect the memory, opinion, or perceptions of those who wrote the reports and gave the testimony. Secondary evidence is innately less trustworthy than primary data simply because it is not specifically verifiable. This procedure also permitted me to compare what various persons reported in the secondary data of reports and testimony. As noted above, inconsistencies were found throughout.

Having shown that Allen's statements, as revealed by the primary tape-recorded interrogations, were consistent throughout but that the written and deposition statements of the police were riddled with assumptions, error, and inconsistencies, I then examined all the records for evidence that the police were overly excited, if not rattled. The following are examples of my findings:

Officer Davis's Deposition Testimony

A: . . . it was obvious that Officer Grayson was a little nervous out here. He's by himself. He didn't know what he had.

Q: Mr. Grayson pretty excited? Fair statement?

A: Yes. Not rattled. I mean just not quite sure what he has yet.

Q: As I look at your report . . . there does not appear to me to be in your report any reference to any footprints other than in the area by the sink and the area by the dining room. . . .

A: Yes. And that's an error of mine . . . what I meant to say . . . what I was meaning was all the firemen tracked an awful lot when they got in there.

A: I'm assuming that when he tells me he ran around the corner that he ran around the patio. He ran at the northeast though.

Q: Your assumption is he ran down the patio?

A: Right.

Q: You had a pretty tough night that night, didn't you?

A: Extremely.

Q: And fair statement to say one of the most difficult nights of your career?

A: Yes.

Q: You had just come from a scene where a young boy had been run over.

A: Yes.

Q: You were visibly shaken before you ever got to this particular scene?

A: Yes . . . inside, yes.

Q: When you finally got home that night, you couldn't sleep?

Q: Right.

911 Operator's Deposition Testimony

Q: . . . it gets real busy down there in a situation like this, doesn't it?

A: Yes, it does.

Q: Would you say you misinterpreted some things he said?

A: Correct.

Officer Grayson's Deposition Testimony

Q: Were you a little excited, Officer, at this particular scene?

A: Yes.

Q: First time you'd been on a homicide, is that correct?

A: Yes.

Q: Had you ever seen a dead body before?

A: Yes.

Q: Had you ever seen a body that had been allegedly beaten with a blunt instrument?

A: What do you mean?

Q: Had you ever seen a crime scene—worked a crime scene like this before?

A: No.

Officer Grayson's Written Report

I found that the front door of the house . . . was closed but unlocked. I do not know if the door was this way when the incident occurred, or as a result of personnel responding to the scene.

I did not see any area on countertops, or the kitchen table top, where it appeared to have been struck with a hammer.

Officer Mason's Deposition Testimony

Q: Are you aware whether or not there were any statements made to police officers prior to the statement you and Officer Potroff took?

A: I don't know about that. . . . I don't know if there was or not.

Q: Was he a suspect when you interviewed him?

A: No, Sir, not at that particular time, he wasn't. I say no. Everybody was a suspect at that time because we really didn't know where to go.

It appears that Defense Attorney Carlson had done a masterful job of eliciting admissions by the officers that they were confused and somewhat rattled. My task was simply to find and organize them in the mass of evidence as a way of explaining why the police were inconsistent. It is important not to give the impression, even with such clear evidence of inconsistency, that the police may have been lying. In such an unusual case, it is natural for police to become rattled, confused, and perhaps even inconsistent. Such a theory offers face saving, whether true or not.

Finally, I tabulated all instances in the deposition testimony of the police, the neighbor, and the 911 operator in which they could not remember facts that one might expect such witnesses to recall, as follows:

Officer Davis Can't Recall

- ▸ how many tracks were present in that blood
- ▸ his exact words to Mr. Allen— . . . did you see the suspect
- ▸ whether one or two Styrofoam cups were on the car
- ▸ whether lights were on outside the house when he arrived
- ▸ where the small dot of blood was on the television screen
- ▸ whether firemen or ambulance people arrived first
- ▸ how the cyclone fence was bent over
- ▸ how he made his report—longhand or dictated
- ▸ where the telephone was located
- ▸ whether bloody footprints were around the bar area
- ▸ when he returned to scene with counsel

Officer Grayson Can't Recall

- ▸ how long before emergency medical personnel arrived
- ▸ where the spot of blood was on the television
- ▸ whether the child was in a green vehicle or blue vehicle
- ▸ what Steve Allen said when he was babbling
- ▸ whether the room had a fireplace
- ▸ whether towels were cloth or paper
- ▸ long period of time after fire people arrived that ambulance people arrived
- ▸ how many ambulance people came
- ▸ whether ambulance people came in through the garage

- whether the washer and dryer were in utility room
- how far blood went beyond the victim's head
- where Davis was while he talked with Allen
- whether fire people had blood on their shoes
- whether something was put down in the blood
- how many officers arrived before Mason
- where his field notes are now
- who the ranking man was on the shift
- at what point Officer Mason arrived in relation to ambulance and fire people
- what his field notes say
- how many pages of field notes he took
- how long a training period he had in securing the scene
- whether they gave him a manual at the police academy on securing a scene

Officer Silver Can't Recall

- the name of the city officer he met at the scene
- whether he got a pulse on Mrs. Allen
- exact words of his question to Allen
- exact words of Allen's answer
- whether or not he asked Allen the race of the intruder
- what Allen said about when he arrived that evening

911 Operator Can't Recall

- when, after the call from Steve Allen, she received a call from 3209 Jefferson Court concerning a black male wearing a white T-shirt
- what her license number is
- the channel designation
- name of person who called at 3209 Jefferson Court

Officer Otte Can't Recall

- exact date he had contact with Allen's clothing
- whether he was gloved or not
- exact words of Allen's statement
- asking Allen what time he made the 911 call
- asking Allen what he did with the paper towels

Officer Mason Can't Recall

- where Allen said the hammer was lying

- ▶ when Allen told him about the hammer
- ▶ whether Allen said the hammer was lying on the floor or on a cabinet
- ▶ whether Gardella's interview was tape-recorded
- ▶ Allen's telling him anywhere else he'd been that evening
- ▶ what time Allen said he'd been at the Sonic
- ▶ whether Allen was read his rights at the 2 a.m. interview
- ▶ name of the medical examiner in Tulsa who told him the hammer was consistent with the wounds to the head
- ▶ Allen telling him that his wife was alive when he found her
- ▶ gender of the three children
- ▶ whether Allen holds an office in the church
- ▶ what day he surrendered himself voluntarily

Neighbor Herring Can't Recall

- ▶ what Grayson said
- ▶ name of the officer he spoke with
- ▶ whether he was asked the same questions in the two interviews
- ▶ how many times he's talked with law enforcement after the first two times
- ▶ whether he wrote his notes after he called Chuck Lowrey
- ▶ whether he told anyone else about the conversation at the funeral home other than Lowrey
- ▶ whether he ever noticed one of the cars not there all night
- ▶ from which direction Allen drove in
- ▶ where Allen went when he exited the car
- ▶ whether he saw Jan Stephenson walking that night
- ▶ perspiration on Allen
- ▶ whether windows were up or down in the car
- ▶ any heat radiating from the car
- ▶ names of baby-sitters
- ▶ words used in alleged verbal abuse by Allen

This analysis, like others before it, grows out of topic analysis—in this case, the topic of not being able to recall. Obviously, it extends the face-saving explanation of police inconsistency based on being rattled and confused and adds the suspicion of incompetence rather than maliciousness.

There can be no question about the confusion at the scene of the crime. Grayson arrived first, followed a minute later by Davis. After that, the sequence of comings and goings is unclear. Fire and ambulance personnel arrived early on, tramping through the area and apparently obliterating clues.

As more and more law enforcement officers arrived, the garage and driveway became filled with people, including various neighbors. Apparently many police officers spoke with Allen. As nearly as can be determined from their reports, their questions had no particular pattern. Police reports involve after-the-fact recall (unless concurrent notes were taken), often days later. When quotations or paraphrases of the suspect are presented, we seldom if ever are told what the investigator said to elicit the statements. Linguists are keenly aware that most questions influence answers, yet investigators seldom include their questions in reports.

It is clear that this investigation was flawed in many other ways as well. Tape recorders malfunctioned during crucial interrogations, including both tape recordings of the interrogations of Allen. To make matters worse, the police allegedly lost the tape of the 3 a.m. interrogation, after a transcript was prepared, offering no way for the defense to check the accuracy of that transcript. Contradictions and inconsistencies abounded both within given reports and testimony as well as across the reports and testimony of the various officers. The police, by their own admission, were at a loss to understand what happened. One explanation of their theory that Allen was the perpetrator is that they had nothing else to go on. If this were the case, one wonders why no effort was made to check out Allen's observation that an intruder was seen leaving the premises. It was, of course, stupid of Allen to hide the hammer in the attic. It was, perhaps, tactless of Allen to avoid talking with his neighbor, although we never learned whether he and that neighbor were close enough to justify such discussion. We also know that a person whose wife has just been found murdered cannot be expected to be in total emotional control. The other alleged evidence of Allen's inconsistency proved to be police investigator inconsistency, as noted above. The case against Allen, therefore, rested on the inferences of the police investigators. The jury did the best they could with what they were given and, in the end, inferred in the same way that the police and prosecutors did, despite the lack of evidence against Allen, and convicted him of murdering his wife. As one freelance writer put it as he left the courtroom, "If ever there was a case of reasonable doubt, it's this one."

▶ Was Chris Jerue Lying?

In the late evening of September 14 or early morning of September 15, 1991, the body of a young man named Frank Corly was found murdered in his Anchorage, Alaska, apartment. Within hours of finding the body, the police strongly suspected 18-year-old Christopher Jerue, whose acquaintance, T. H. (a female minor), had already explained to the police that Chris had bragged to her about his involvement, telling her, "We shot somebody." Armed with this lead, the Anchorage police got T. H. to make a telephone call to Chris to get him to repeat what she claims he told her. This call was covertly tape-recorded. Unfortunately for the police, this conversation revealed no direct admissions by Jerue, although he did ask T. H. "not to say anything to anyone about it."

Jerue and a friend, Lavon S. (a male minor), were seen riding bicycles stolen from Corly's home after his murder. The police stopped them at a grocery store and discovered a loaded .22 revolver in the possession of Lavon, who was subsequently detained. T. H. had run into them at the grocery store and, at Jerue's request, rode one of the two bicycles to Jerue's home for him. She claims that, en route, Jerue had admitted to the crime.

Not satisfied with the fruits of T. H.'s telephone call with Jerue, the police arranged for another friend, Jennifer Wilson, to visit Jerue at his home. She was wearing a body microphone. In this conversation, Jerue first denies any involvement, but Jennifer persists, asking, "Why did you have to kill him?" Jerue responds that the victim was "a faggot who tried to hit on them" and that Lavon S. had a gun and shot him. Jerue also admits to robbing Corly afterward. Jennifer continues, "I can't believe you guys killed somebody," to which Jerue responds, "Hey, he did it, I didn't do shit." The tape mysteriously goes off for an unspecified amount of time and then comes back on with a knocking on the door. Jerue and Jennifer are now at Lavon's house to pick him up and drive him to the airport. Jennifer finally tells both Chris and Lavon that she wants to hear the story of what really happened. Lavon then describes in detail how he shot Corly in the head.

Armed with Jennifer's tape, the police then picked up Lavon and Jerue and interrogated Jerue 4 days later. This interrogation framed whatever case the defense could muster. Clearly, Jerue was with Lavon when the latter killed Corly. Clearly, their intent was to rob the victim. Clearly, they stole some loose change, a sweater, a bottle of cologne, a pair of Reebok shoes, and two bicycles. At issue, however, was their intent to murder and whether Jerue was an accomplice to the killing.

Intent to Murder

Police efforts to get Jerue to admit that he and Lavon had planned to kill Corly were couched in the verb *know:*

- "You already *knew* what you were gonna do when you went back over to the apartment?"
- "You *knew* that before you even went back over there, right?"
- "You *knew* what you were gonna do before you even got there. Both you and Lavon."

The verb *know* has several meanings, according to most dictionaries:

- to have understanding of or be acquainted with
- to have experienced
- to be acquainted with
- to be aware of the truth or factuality of
- to be convinced or certain

But one can also say things like, "I know that Jones is going to win the election," or, "I know it's going to rain tomorrow when we have our picnic." Such sentences connote more than the above dictionary meanings of *know*. Instead, they indicate predictions, suspicions, or speculations.

Jerue's responses to these questions that used the verb *know* were as follows:

- "No."
- "Yeah, but I didn't know he was gonna shoot him though."
- "We didn't plan to kill him when we were goin' over there."

Jerue clearly denies intent to murder when the police ask the question using the verb *know*.

The interrogators also tried to get at intent by using other words, as follows:

Interrogators' Questions	Jerue's Responses
1. You guys intended to go over there and rob him and kill him, didn't you?	No, we didn't plan to kill him at all.
2. But it was an understanding and a plan between the two of you for him to do it, right?	Yeah.
3. You both planned to do it—before—up to 2 hours before you and Lavon actually shot him, you both planned on shootin' him, right?	Right.

Interrogators' Questions	Jerue's Responses
4. OK, that's what we thought, and you just had to kill him to rip his stuff off.	No, we were just gonna hold him at gunpoint, that's what I thought.
5. But about 2 hours before he actually shot him is when he changed your mind and decided to shoot him, right?	Right.
6. Then, if I understand you right, you guys changed your mind from robbin' him to shootin' him about 2 hours before he actually shot him, right?	Yeah, about that, yeah.
7. That's when both of you changed your mind, you both agreed on it at that point, right?	Right.

At this point, things do not look good for Chris Jerue. He had responded negatively to the interrogator's use of *intended,* but when he agreed that there was a plan between them, he may well have been confused about what the interrogator referred to when he used the word *it.* Clearly, Jerue and Lavon planned to rob Corly. Less favorable to Jerue is his agreement to the third proposition—"2 hours before you and Lavon actually shot him, you both planned on shootin' him." Or was it? In the fourth statement, Jerue denies that they planned to kill Corly. What could cause Jerue to jump back and forth between disagreement and agreement that the killing was planned? One answer is that he did not catch the full force of what the interrogators were saying. In Statement 3, Jerue may well have been saying "Right" to the part of the question mentioning 2 hours.

Building on this small but inconsistent advance toward confession, the police continue with Question 5. It is difficult to know what Jerue was agreeing with here because the question is so infelicitous. What they meant by "he changed your mind and decided to shoot him" is far from clear, but it is not inconceivable that Jerue translated the infelicitous "he changed your mind and decided to shoot him" to "he changed his mind and decided to shoot him." Evidence for this reading of the question is bolstered by the police officer's omission of any possessive pronoun at all before the verb *decided.* If the interrogator merely misspoke with his use of "your mind," he doubly confounded potential understanding of what he meant by not saying who (he or you) "decided to shoot him."

Perhaps sensing the ambiguity about who planned or intended what, the interrogator restates his proposition in Question 6, this time disambiguating with the words, "you guys changed your mind." It would have been a clearer case against Jerue if the interrogator had ended his question before adding "about 2 hours before he actually shot him." Jerue's response, though beginning with an affirmative "Yeah," gives clear indication that he focused his answer on the "2 hours" part of the question, rather than on the "you guys changed your mind" part of the question. His "Yeah, about that, yeah" provides such evidence. Virtually all published advice to law enforcement officers who interrogate suspects tells them to limit their questions to simple sentences, not compound or complex ones, to avoid possible misinterpretations or misunderstandings that could later be in dispute.

Perhaps realizing that he still didn't have the confession he wanted, the interrogator restates his question one more time, in Question 7 above. This appears to be the confirmation he wanted, and Jerue once again responds affirmatively. Closer examination of this question, however, reveals that it is virtually identical with Question 6, concluding with the time reference "at that point," which refers to the "about 2 hours" noted in his Question 6. If Jerue was following the _recency principle,_ responding to the most recent proposition in a sequence of propositions, we can learn only that Jerue agreed that it was about 2 hours before Corly was shot that Lavon decided to kill rather than just rob the man.

A skeleton summary of this series of questions and answers may focus the issues more clearly here:

Question	Answer
1. You both intended to kill him?	No.
2. You both planned to do it?	Yeah.
3. You both planned it 2 hours before Lavon shot him?	Yeah.
4. You had to kill him to rob him?	No.
5. Two hours before he changed your mind and decided to shoot him?	Right.
6. You guys changed your mind 2 hours before he shot him?	Yeah, about that.
7. You changed your mind, both agreed on it, at that point?	Right.

Questions 1 and 4 focus on the word *kill*. Jerue strongly disagrees with both questions. Questions 2, 3, and 7 focus on the word *it*. To these questions, Jerue is affirmative in his response. Questions 3, 5, 6, and 7 contain time references, to which Jerue is also affirmative.

On the surface, it would appear that Jerue is giving conflicting answers to the police about his intent. But a careful analysis of the interrogator's questioning sequence provides some explanation for Jerue's apparent inconsistency.

Questioning is an art that is highly developed by professionals. To the interrogators, Jerue fits Inbau et al.'s (1986, pp. 77-194) profile of suspects who are believed to be guilty. Although we cannot say for certain that these interrogators deliberately tried to trick Jerue into admitting his intent to commit the murder, their questions give some support to that idea. The question sequence is similar to that used by salespersons trying to persuade customers to purchase. If sellers do not elicit a yes to their propositions, they reframe the issue in words that can elicit yes answers. In this case, the first reframe was to replace "kill" with the less specific "do it." Because Jerue had already admitted that he had planned to rob Corly, the interrogator's "do it" might well have represented robbery to him, especially because he had just denied intent to kill. For verification purposes, the interrogator then re-asks the "do it" question, this time adding the time frame at the end. Again, Jerue responds affirmatively but consistently with his previous answer to the "do it" question.

Perhaps encouraged or emboldened, the interrogator pays a return visit to the "kill" question, believing, no doubt, that Jerue had recanted his earlier no. Jerue's answer to Question 4, however, was consistent with his answer to Question 1, the first "kill" question. So far, then, we can conclude either that Jerue was flipping back and forth about his premeditation to kill Corly or, more realistically, that he had thus far interpreted Questions 2 and 3 to be about planned robbery.

Question 5 is somewhat distinctive. Here, the interrogator builds on the time focus (2 hours before) and then utters the infelicitous "he changed your mind" (with stress on the word *he*). It is not difficult to understand how a listener might have expected to hear "he convinced you" or "you changed your mind" if the question were to indicate that Jerue's intentions changed. Instead, he hears "he changed your mind," with heavy stress on *he* and light stress on *your*. But there is more. The sentence continues "and decided to shoot him." Previous stress on the pronoun *he* marks *he* as the subject of this sentence. The question contains a compound verb: *changed* and *decided*. Whatever significance Jerue may have attached to "he changed your mind," it is indisputable that *he* governs "decided to shoot him." When Jerue responds affirmatively, he is agreeing that something changed 2 hours before and that he (Lavon) decided to shoot Corly.

Apparently, the interrogators recognized some ambiguity remaining, so they asked the question once more as Question 6. This time, the subject and pronoun match, "You guys changed your mind." This part of the question is followed by the time reference, "2 hours before he shot him." Jerue's affirmative response to this question would be devastating to his case except for one thing—the way he responded: "Yeah, about that," which has less logical reference to "you guys changed your mind" but perfect logical reference to "2 hours before he shot him." To this point, Jerue could well have felt comfortable with the belief that he had been utterly clear that they had both planned a robbery but had not planned a murder. He was equally comfortable, he thought, that he had made it clear that about 2 hours before the shooting, Lavon had changed his own mind and decided to kill Corly.

Seeking confirmation for what they considered an admission by Jerue that he had, indeed, planned Corly's death 2 hours prior to the shooting, the interrogators ask Question 6 over again, as Question 7. If ever there was an opportunity to up the ante, it was here. Now would have been the time to use the word *kill*. But instead, the police back off, returning to the less precise *it*. Likewise, the structure of the presumed validation question is exactly the same as that of Question 6, the one it was to validate. Good interrogation advice and practice are to ask the validating question in a different way, with more precision and more clarity. These interrogators violated such advice. Jerue's response to Question 6 was to the time focus of the question, as noted above. Because Question 7 contained no structural change, one can assume that Jerue was engaging in his own form of validation, agreeing with the same answer he gave to Question 6.

A topic/response flow chart of this sequence of crucial questions concerning Jerue's premeditation is as follows:

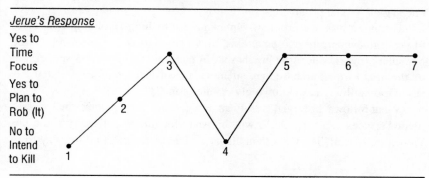

Jerue's Response

Yes to Time Focus

Yes to Plan to Rob (It)

No to Intend to Kill

Chris Jerue was clearly guilty of a great many things, including robbery. It was equally clear that he did not kill Corly. The most important issue for him at his trial was whether he, along with Lavon, intended to murder Corly before the killing took place. The major evidence used by the prosecution included the above interrogation questions and answers. Because he was penniless, he was given a court-appointed Anchorage attorney, Glen Cravez. Cravez sought my assistance but was unable to secure funds for my presence at trial. I presented my analysis to him via telephone, fax, and Federal Express, but he was unable to present it in its most effective way, and Jerue was convicted of aiding in the planned murder of Frank Corly.

► Did Donald Goltz Believe What He Confessed?

The far extent to which law enforcement will go in eliciting a confession may have been established in the case of *United States v. Donald Goltz*. Goltz,[1] a local judge, also served as a nonpaid member of the Havre, Montana, Airport Authority. The airport was a source of community pride, but it operated on few or no budget resources.

Controversy arose over the purchase of government surplus property. The airport needed a four-wheel-drive tractor to clear snow from the runway, and the airport authority thought it found a solution on the surplus list. As it turns out, the payloader was in bad shape, but, no matter, the authority board had no money for it anyway. The airport manager, Bill Gorton, said he could fix up the tractor and put up his own money to pay for it, adding that if the airport authority wanted it later, they could have it. This statement complicated matters somewhat, but it seemed like a doable solution to the board. It seemed sensible to have an attorney record the transaction officially, but because lawyers cost money, the board was not able to follow this procedure. Judge Goltz then decided to draw up the lease on behalf of the board, and things once again looked promising.

But there was one problem. Unbeknownst to Judge Goltz, the purchase of government surplus equipment includes a stipulation that one cannot lease out such property once it is purchased. In fact, this stipulation is spelled out on the back of the purchase agreement. It is clear that the judge violated this stipulation although not knowingly or intentionally.

What follows, however, is truly amazing. Some 3 years later, the Government Services Agency (GSA) was informed of this violation by some unknown individual. The GSA then dispatched an investigator all the way from

Texas to get to the bottom of things in Havre, Montana. He learned that nobody profited from this procedural error, but he nevertheless pursued an investigation of all concerned parties. Central to his investigation were interviews of Judge Goltz, Sylvia Kraft (the authority secretary), board member Bob Stimson, and Airport Manager Bill Gorton. The interviews were not tape-recorded. Instead, GSA Investigator Byron Murray got each interviewee to produce a handwritten statement, allegedly reflecting the contents of each session. The statements of Judge Goltz and Bill Gorton were tantamount to confession statements.

The attorney for Judge Goltz, Ron Reeves, naturally was puzzled about what kind of defense he could mount for his client when no tape recordings and no reports or notes of the meetings were made available. He did the next logical thing: He sent his investigator, Hal Timmons, to interview these same people in an effort to reconstruct what they and Agent Murray actually said during the interrogations that produced their handwritten statements. Especially puzzling were Murray's two interviews with Judge Goltz, a month apart, which were diametrically different in content and tone. In the first statement, on January 13, 1993, for example, Judge Goltz writes ". . . The agreement dated Aug. 16, 1990, was not in compliance with Federal Surplus Property regulations, irregardless [*sic*] of the intent and circumstances and purposes for which this property was acquired." On his second interview, on February 10, 1993, Judge Goltz produced a strikingly different statement, which included words and phrases such as "I have not complied," "violations," "illegal," "fraudulently," "misrepresentation," and "perpetration of the unlawful acts." No mention was made of intent, circumstances, or purposes for acquiring the tractor in the second statement, which reads like a confession.

The interviews of Reeves's investigator with the other parties gave clues to why Judge Goltz moved from a focus on intent to a mournful admission of misrepresentation, fraud, and crime. Authorities on police interrogation advocate that the suspect's statements be tape-recorded; that no type, manner, or kind of compulsion be produced by the interrogator; that the suspect be permitted to go through a confession narrative without interruption; that the interrogator take notes during a retelling of this narrative; that the confession statement be typed up immediately after it is made and then be presented to the suspect for authentication; and that the interrogator avoid "leading" the suspect in what to say or how to say it.

From the reports of investigator Hal Timmons, it is apparent that Agent Murray chose not to follow these standard procedures. One of his techniques was described by Sheriff Ralph Tobins, the witness to these interrogations, as "co-mingling." By "co-mingling," Sheriff Tobins explained that Agent Murray stopped the interviews in various places and asked the subjects to write out what they had just said. After accomplishing this, the interrogation was resumed, only to be interrupted again with the writing-down exercise. The sheriff noted that Murray followed this procedure consistently in all his interviews. Sheriff Tobins's description was verified by the others interviewed by the agent. However such a technique may be evaluated by law enforcement, it flies in the face of basic principles in the construction of a narrative, wherein each sentence created by a writer foreshadows the sentences to come next. From the agent's technique, as described by witnesses, only Agent Murray had a sense of the unfolding direction of the independently constructed sentences. That he "knew" where the statements were leading is evident by the claims of witnesses that he caused them to reword their statements in various ways. The ultimate products of these statements provide little evidence that Agent Murray was motivated by any overwhelming desire for grammatical appropriateness or style. It is apparent that his intent was to cause the subjects to produce statements that matched his own goals. His style of interrogation is similar to that used by attorneys with witnesses in a trial, building whole pictures from bits and pieces at a time, with the goal of constructing a product of their own advocacy preference, whether or not the witness shares that perspective. Law enforcement interrogation, conventionally at least, avoids such advocacy and does not decontextualize the subject's narrative to suit the interrogator's goals. Interrogation is a descriptive process, not advocacy; it is a fact-finding process, not a litigation.

When interrogators choose to cause the subject to handwrite his or her own statement, they face certain difficulties. Aubry and Caputo (1980) describe these difficulties as follows:

> The disadvantages of the handwritten confession are many and include the fact that some people write in almost illegible handwriting. Another major disadvantage is the fact that the handwritten confession is usually a very slow, laborious, tedious, and cumbersome procedure; and that the subject will have to be "led" in the actual making of the confession. However, if he is "led" in the making of a confession, then the confession is obviously not his own free and completely voluntary statement. If he is not 'led', but left entirely to his own devices in actually authoring the statement, the chances are excellent that material details, facts, incidents, circumstances, and background information will either be omitted or inadequately covered. (p. 325)

The very "slow, laborious, tedious and cumbersome" process to which Aubry and Caputo (1980) refer also highlights the decontextualized nature of the technique selected by Agent Murray. The writing process, like the talking process, represents a continuous flow of interconnected ideas. This interconnectedness explains why experts on interrogation recommend that a suspect be permitted to tell his or her whole story, without interruption, at least once. When writers (in this case, a suspect) are continuously stopped and are asked to word things differently, train of thought is blocked while they are focused on the specific individual words at issue; that is, they may agree with the logic and wording of the individual words without considering the impact such individual items will have on the entire narrative. Thus, the compiling of individual sentences in this manner can suit the intent of the interrogator but thwart the intent of the writer.

The issue of intention, therefore, is crucial in the construction of the whole statement. The interrogator's intention in this case is revealed by the technique he chose to use—the "co-mingling" of the subjects' individual answers with Murray's request for them to then write them down before resuming the oral interview. Starkly contrastive to Murray's approach is that advocated by experts in law enforcement interrogation, who suggest (a) tape-recording the interrogation to dispel any hints of coercion (Inbau et al., 1986, pp. 176-178; Nissman et al., 1985, p. 349), (b) presenting the typed-up statement to the subject for authentication and signature immediately after the interview (Aubry & Caputo, 1980, p. 322; Inbau et al., 1986, p. 180), (c) not interrupting the narrative (Nissman et al., 1985, p. 332), and (d) not attempting to improve the language of the subject (Aubry & Caputo, 1980, p. 325; Inbau et al., 1986, p. 184). On this latter point, Woods (1990) says, "The best course of action is probably to suggest the individual making the statement write it out himself in his own words and without prompting" (p. 140). Aubry and Caputo (1980) elaborate on the concept of restraint in obtaining confessions, arguing that *restraint* (an act, process, or means of restraining; a restraining force or *influence*) will invalidate the confession: "Restraint is also thought of as the establishing of control over someone's thoughts or feelings, or the expression of those thoughts or feelings. 'Restrain' is defined as 'to draw back, to check, to repress or suppress, to limit or restrict" (pp. 314-315). Therefore, any influence Murray had on causing subjects to omit or restrict what they had said orally in their written statements falls under the heading of "restraint."

Building a statement or confession in the manner evidenced here by Agent Murray is similar to the technique used in constructing a documentary film. The producer or director can, in such instances, select and edit at will toward the goal of yielding a product that suits his or her own intended outcome. Documentary filmmaking comes closer to the procedures to be used at trial than to procedures that are acceptable as the fact-finding evidence elicited in statements. Sheriff Tobins's own words support the claim that Agent Murray did not follow the guidelines of acceptable interrogation:

- ► "He told them what he was looking for and asked for it in their own handwriting."
- ► "He explained to them what he was looking for in the affidavit."
- ► "He told them what he wanted in the affidavit."
- ► "Murray was telling them what he wanted written down in connection with what he wanted it to do with the topic."
- ► "When something they said that Murray felt was relevant, he asked them to write it in the affidavit."

The Airport Authority Board secretary, Sylvia Kraft, supported Sheriff Tobins on this point:

- ► "If I said something good about Donald, he didn't want me to write anything like that down. He wanted me to write down something that would implicate him in the whole thing. That's the only thing he wanted me to write down."
- ► "Murray would tell me: 'I don't want to put words in your mouth'. But then he told me things to put down . . . He'd more or less dictate what I wrote . . . He said if there's anything else you want to put down, put it in your own words. But before I'd put it down, he'd want to hear what I had to say."

Bob Stimson also supported Sheriff Tobins and Sylvia Kraft on this point:

- ► "Well, he was after certain statements I supposed that he wanted to get."
- ► "He would kind of suggest how he wanted it worded. Or he'd ask it in a different way, until he possibly got the answers he was looking for."
- ► "My feeling is he wouldn't have quit until he got what he wanted."

Clues to the intention of Judge Goltz are also evident from his two handwritten statements. His January 13, 1993, statement, for example, is replete with indefinite, tentative beliefs and intentions, as the following illustrate:

- ► "Conflicts which *may have* arisen if I continued to serve on the Board . . ."
- ► "Based upon the documents presented to me, which *were claimed* to be the full and complete records . . ."
- ► "*I do not believe* the Havre Airport Authority records will show . . ."

▶ "Upon review of distribution Doc. #09394, and further education, that agreement contained thereon dated Aug. 16, 1990 was not in compliance with Federal Surplus Property regulations, irregardless of the intent and circumstances and purposes for which this property was acquired."

On February 10, 1993, a second statement by Judge Goltz is starkly different. It contains no indefinite, tentative beliefs or intentions. If Agent Murray had followed acceptable interrogation procedures and tape-recorded the interviews in which these statements were elicited, we might well have the answer to why these two statements by Judge Goltz are so different. Obviously, Agent Murray had not achieved his goal with the first interrogation; otherwise, there would have been no need for a second one. In that Judge Goltz includes words and phrases such as "I have not complied," "violations," "illegal," "fraudulently," "misrepresentation," and "perpetration of the unlawful acts" in his second statement but not in his first, something clearly brought about this change in wording. In the light of what Sheriff Tobins, Sylvia Kraft, and Bob Stimson report about the influence of Agent Murray in the wording of the statements, one answer is obvious: Agent Murray probably led Judge Goltz, as he led the others, in what to say, as well as in what not to say. If this is the case, the issue of whether these statements were their own free and voluntary words is in question.

The case against Judge Goltz remained in legal limbo for many months, causing the judge great anxiety and embarrassment. Meanwhile, determined discussions continued between the prosecutor and Attorney Reeves. Possibly as a result of these discussion, which revealed much of the above analysis, the prosecutor decided not to indict Judge Goltz.

Recent research on the coercive nature of some police interrogations shows how an innocent person can be influenced to admit guilt. Kassin's study (Kassin & Sukel, 1997), presented at the 1995 meeting of the American Psychological Association and reported in the October 1995 issue of *APA Monitor* (Azar, 1995), had 75 college students participate in an experiment. The students were asked to type letters, read by a clandestine research confederate, as quickly as possible. They were warned, first, not to press a specific key, which would cause the computer to crash, losing the data. After a minute, each computer was automatically rigged to crash, and the confederate immediately accused the typist of pressing the forbidden key. Videotapes of the process made it clear that none of the subjects actually did this, and at first each denied it. Kassin then asked the subjects to sign a prepared statement of guilt while the confederate claimed that he saw the subjects actually press the key. If they refused to sign after two requests, they received an angry telephone call from Kassin. Eventually, almost two thirds of the subjects signed the statement. A further step was also taken to determine feelings of guilt. Another student confederate waited outside the room where the accusations took place, easily overhearing the shouting. The experimenter then left the subject alone with the new confederate, taping the ensuing conversation. Over half of the subjects admitted their guilt to the confederate. If this were not enough, the subjects were then brought back into the lab and were asked to reconstruct their actions; 35% reported they had hit the key with the side of their hand even though the videotape record makes it clear that they did not. Kassin concluded that innocent people can be induced to internalize their guilt and that the use of false evidence increases this risk. Interestingly, law enforcement officers can legally introduce such false evidence.

► Some Problems With Police Interrogation

Perhaps the major problem with handbooks on interrogation is that they are reductionist in orientation. The following list of clues to deception is offered by MacDonald and Michaud (1992, pp. 36-38):

Brief answers
Excessively delayed answers
Repeating the question
Rephrasing the question
Hesitation in answering
Memory problems
Qualified answers
References to honesty
References to religion
Softening terms of violence and theft
Speaking in the third person
Overpoliteness or irritability
Short-lived anger

However accurate any of these clues to deception might be, finding exceptions to the authors' overclaim for them as indicators of a suspect's intent to lie is relatively easy. Contrary to what MacDonald and Michaud state, for example, the suspect who gives only brief answers is not almost certainly lying through concealment of information. The interrogator needs to know considerably more than this clue might provide. For example, one needs a baseline of the suspect's normal answering style, as well as information about his or her background that would tell whether or not he or she becomes brief while under pressure, anxiety, or fear.

Suspects who give detailed answers to questions that the interrogator believes do not require elaboration may well be specialists in these areas and, like most of us, leap at the chance to elaborate about things they know (see Chapter 8 for an example).

A person who repeats the question may not be just stalling for time but, rather, may be a perfectionist who wants to be certain he or she heard the question properly. Likewise, rephrasing the question can be considered a cooperative effort by the suspect to make sure he or she is on the same wavelength with the questioner.

Hesitation in answering can follow an individual and cultural speaking style and is not necessarily deceptive. The use of pause fillers, such as *um* and *uh,* may merely reflect the suspect's search for the best way of saying something; the fillers are not necessarily deceptive in themselves.

Memory problems are endemic to the human condition. If MacDonald and Michaud's (1992) list is to be taken seriously, much of the deposition and trial testimony of police officers would have to be taken as deceptive (e.g., see the memory problems listed in this chapter for Officers Davis, Grayson, Silver, Otte, and Mason in the Allen case).

Qualified answers are the trademark of academics and others who know enough not to make unqualified statements. If this is deceptive behavior, then most academics and well-educated people must be considered liars.

Those who commonly say things like "to tell you the truth," "frankly," and "I swear to God" often do so out of habit, as a common ritual in their conversations. I once uttered the words "to be perfectly honest with you" to the prosecutor while on the stand. He took the opportunity to remind me that I was under oath and was expected to be honest. This admonition, was, of course, all for jury effect, and to be perfectly honest, I haven't used that expression much since.

It is difficult to know why references to religion are considered deceptive. Religious people tend to talk about religion and to use religious terms. MacDonald and Michaud (1992) claim this use raises suspicion because of the inappropriate context in which these comments are made. One person's appropriate context is, apparently, another person's inappropriate context. To a deeply religious person, all contexts are appropriate.

Softening terms are also perplexing. Some people soften violence in their references to it; others do not. Some are given to euphemisms; others are not. But to say that an innocent suspect will say, "I didn't murder him," whereas a guilty one will say, "I didn't hurt him," taxes the very credibility of this list.

Likewise, using the third person instead of the first person is said to be a bad sign. Thus, "It is possible that he could have done that" is considered deceptive, as though the suspect wants to distance him- or herself from the interrogation and from the crime. What this overlooks, of course, is that the speaker may well be referring to someone else, not to him- or herself. And, by the way, who in an interrogation wouldn't want to distance him- or herself from the interrogation and the crime, especially if that person is innocent?

Overpoliteness, such as saying, "Do you mind if I say something, Sir?" is also considered a sign of deceitful language. By the same token, so is being hypercritical, such as the suspect's asking, "I've already talked to one detective. Do I have to go over this again?" Apparently, any extreme of emotion leads a speaker to invite suspicion. The clear message is to be blah, non-emotional, and calm despite the fact that the person is a suspect brought before the police for interrogation of a crime. This message is, of course, unrealistic and underlines the naïveté of any law enforcement officer who believes it.

Short-lived anger is the last "clue" in MacDonald and Michaud's list of deceptive language behaviors. These authors say that both the innocent and the guilty will express rage at first but that the innocent will persevere in the anger, whereas the guilty party will become calmer. Just how this clue correlates with the preceding clue of hypercritical language is left unresolved.

One problem with this list (and others as well) is that even though it may contain germs of truth, it is reductionist in philosophy. This is not to say that some law enforcement officers are not good at spotting deception. They may well be very good at it. The problem comes in trying to isolate the clues and teach others to use them. I suspect that the authors of this list would agree that even though any one of these features is present, the suspect may, indeed, be innocent. Does a clustering of such features provide the effective interrogator with the clues needed to make a judgment? If so, which cluster and how many clues are enough for a considered decision? Even the effective techniques of Avinoam Sapir (1987), at his Laboratory for Scientific Investigation in Phoenix, claim only to narrow down the list of suspects for eventual interrogation. Sapir's work, discussed elsewhere in this book, makes use of language clues to deceptive behavior that provide the interrogator with specific areas in which the interview can focus attention.

Another problem with such a list of clues is that we don't know whether the interrogator first has an idea of truth or deception and then looks for clues in verbal and nonverbal behavior to justify that idea or whether these clues create an idea of truth or deception. One would hope it is the latter, but one probably suspects it is the former. If the clues are discovered to support a preexistent idea of deception, then the pressure is on the verifiability of that idea; that is, the idea needs to be analyzed and verified by itself. If the idea of deception is first conceived through information outside the interrogation and then the language clues are used to support or disconfirm that information, then the procedure may have some merit, but only if the language clues are felicitous. The set of language clues offered by most manuals are, as noted above, highly questionable. If the idea of deception is first conceived by these language clues, the problem is even greater because they are also questionable.

The case of Steve Allen is illustrative. From the evidence made available in this case, it appears likely that the original idea of his guilt came from the belief by law enforcement officers that the person who discovers the body and reports the matter is most likely the killer. It appears that the police then searched for language evidence through his interrogations, 911 call, and conversations with a neighbor to support this idea. Had the police begun their intelligence analysis with the language Allen used in these verbal encounters, they would have been hard-pressed to reach the same conclusion. To do so would have seemed ludicrous because the features they found were so inconclusive.

Thus, we can learn that language indicators of deception are, at best, merely support features to an already formed idea. This is so because the only conclusive language evidence of deception is found in the suspect's inconsistency of statements, not in his or her manner of speaking. The major inconsistencies in the Allen case were produced by those who were not the suspect: the police, the 911 operator, and the neighbor. The language used by law enforcement officers was central in another way in the Jerue and Goltz cases, misleading and leading, respectively. For reasons perhaps natural and predictable, at trial the main focus of the interrogations is placed by the prosecution on the defendant's language but by the defense on the language of the interrogators and the accusers. The prosecution traditionally narrows in on veracity and deception, whereas the defense examines consistency in the defendant's answers and the misleading nature or ambiguity of the interrogator's questions. Needless to say, the defense has better ground to stand on because deceptive language is, at best, unscientifically presented and impossible to prove from our current knowledge base, whereas consistency or inconsistency of answers and misleading questions stand on a more solid linguistic foundation of proof.

The three cases involving multiple interrogations discussed in this chapter were flawed in numerous ways. How might these flaws have been avoided? Available guides to police interrogation, such as Inbau et al. (1986), MacDonald and Michaud (1992), Aubry and Caputo (1980), Woods (1990), Kamisar (1980), and Yeschke (1987), offer little more than broad advice, such as asking only one question at a time, allowing the suspect to first tell his or her story without interruption, asking clear questions, choosing words carefully, rephrasing for validation, and avoiding yes-no questions. These guides also suggest various strategies or tactics to elicit confession (e.g., see Inbau et al.'s suggestions about "themes" to be developed, such as sympathizing that such behavior is normal, condemning others, appealing to pride [1986, Chap. 6]). In all fairness, many of these works were prepared as practical manuals for police officers and are not linguistically motivated.

The Allen case is a classic example of a bungled investigation with lost tapes, malfunctioning equipment, a poorly supervised crime scene, mistaken hearing, failed recall of the officers, and suspect evidence. The Jerue case gives evidence of unskillful questioning techniques, along with questionable inferences by the officers of what Jerue was saying. The Goltz case gives clear indication of the interrogator's hand in constructing the alleged confession that he had apparently dictated. Careful analysis of the language used in the interrogations sheds considerable light on these cases.

► **Note**

1. The names have been changed in this account to protect the anonymity of the innocent.

Language and Constitutional Rights

The primary law governing eliciting confessions is that the confessor voluntarily acknowledge his or her guilt. In 1943 and 1944, the Supreme Court ruled in *McNabb v. United States* (318 U.S. 332, 1943): "Not only must a confession be voluntary and trustworthy, but it must also have been obtained by 'civilized' interrogation procedure" (Inbau et al., 1986, p. 247).[1] The Court held that any person arrested should be taken before a U.S. commissioner or a federal judge without delay. If a confession were obtained during a period of delay, it would be deemed inadmissible.

In 1958, Congress introduced a bill that provided that no statement or confession would be admissible as evidence in a federal case solely because of any reasonable delay in taking the arrested person before a federal commissioner or judge. In 1966, in *Miranda v. Arizona,* the Supreme Court mandated that warnings of constitutional rights were prerequisite to the interrogation of suspects. The basis of this decision was the Court's goal to make suspects aware of their self-incrimination privilege. Even though the Constitution provided that nobody should be forced to be a witness against him- or herself, no statute provided that police interrogators were actually required to warn a suspect of the right to remain silent. In addition to the warning about self-incrimination, *Miranda* also required that suspects be advised of their right to counsel before and during the interrogation and that only with a "knowing and intelligent" waiver of these rights could the interrogation take place. The specific wording in *Miranda* concerning these rights was that the suspect had a right to remain silent, and that he need not answer any questions. That if he does answer questions, his answers can be used as evidence against him. That he has a right to consult with a lawyer before or during the questioning of him by the police. That if he cannot afford to hire a lawyer, one will be provided for him without cost.

Interrogators were not required to use these precise words but were mandated to convey these basic rights to the suspect. Commonly, police officers carry a card on which the following is typical:

1. You have the right to remain silent.
2. Anything you say can and will be used against you in a court of law.
3. You have the right to talk with a lawyer and have him or her present with you while you are being questioned.
4. If you cannot afford to hire a lawyer, one will be appointed to represent you before any questioning, if you wish.
5. You may decide at any time to exercise these rights and not answer any questions or make any statements.

At this point, the police officer then attempts to obtain the suspect's waiver of rights by asking:

1. Do you understand each of these rights?
2. Having these rights in mind, do you wish to talk to us now?

These questions attempt to ensure that the suspect has comprehended the statement of rights.

▶ *Miranda* Rights in the DWI Arrest

However much one may applaud the government in its effort to ensure that suspects know and understand their rights, virtually any linguist can find flaws in the procedure commonly used to implement the *Miranda* warnings.

Reading the Rights Aloud

For example, in 1987 I was given videotapes of nine DWI (driving while intoxicated) arrests in Dallas.[2] These interviews make it clear that the officers' major concern was to follow the prescribed form written on the plastic cards provided by the department. Three statements were read to suspects: (a) their rights, (b) their being placed under arrest, and (c) their request to sign any refusal to take a Breathalyzer test. The first problem posed by this procedure of following the prescribed form exactly is that listener comprehension takes second place to accurate police performance. The second problem is that the officers in this brief sample were neither accomplished readers nor able performers. Reading ineffectiveness on the part of the reader contributes to comprehension failure on the part of the person being read to. The following excerpt is illustrative:

> I have requested that you give me a specimen of your breaf. I have inform you of the subsequence, of the consequence of, of not givin' a specimen. . . . The driver's license, the operating driver's license the privilege of operatin' a motor vehicle will be automatically suspended 30 days for period of 90 days after notice and hearing.

After the second sentence, the subject asked, "Could you repeat that? Consequences of not givin' my *test*?" He apparently heard *test* for *breaf*. The subject obviously did not understand the officer's reading. It is difficult to know how the subject comprehended the third sentence because the suspension of 30 days for a period of 90 days is, at best, incomprehensible.

One major characteristic of the DWI arrest event is that subjects frequently request clarification. The officers are generally polite in their responses but not very informative. (One subject, named Jody, requested clarification at least 10 times during one part of his interview.) Requests for clarification received one of three basic responses: (a) "What didn't you understand?"; (b) "I already explained that"; or (c) rereading the exact words read earlier.

To ask a person what he or she doesn't understand is a journey toward futility. In the field of education, it is gradually being recognized that one major problem students face is that they do not know what it is they do not know. Therefore, their efforts to express their problems are incoherent, if not hopeless. Although the officer's question "What don't you understand?" seems, on the surface, to be rational and polite, it is, in reality, a rather foolish question.

Occasionally, the subject managed an attempt to say what he or she didn't understand. In one instance, for example, Jody and his officer had the following dialogue:

Jody: I don't understand.

Officer: What don't you understand?

Jody: The middle section, about me givin' up a specimen.

Officer: I already explained that to you.

This response is equivalent to the impatient parent's explanation to a child's request: "Why do I have to got to bed?" Answer: "Because." This answer is no answer at all and communicates nothing.

The most common response to a request for clarification, however, is to reread the exact words read earlier. The futility of this procedure is obvious. If the subject did not understand the first time the words were read, there is little likelihood that a second reading will cause any improvement. The assumption underlying exact repetition, in fact, is that the subject has not heard the response. But if he or she had not heard it, the subject is not likely to say, "I don't understand it." Rather, he or she would say, "What?" "Huh?" "I didn't hear you," or even, "Would you repeat that?" One of the most obvious strategies used for clarification is rephrasing the same concept in different terms. Such a strategy is not common in the DWI interviews I analyzed, and the absence of such a strategy again suggests that the officers are primarily concerned with getting through the event without getting into trouble; they avoid using "unapproved" language or freelancing off the prescribed pathway.

Sequential Ordering of the Rights

The *Miranda* legislation prescribed neither the exact words to be used nor the sequence in which the points should be presented. The situation is quite similar to that of the Federal Trade Commission's (FTC) regulations for warning labels on hazardous products: Certain things must be said, but how these statement are to be worded and the order in which they are to appear are left to the manufacturer, except for one major difference. The FTC also often includes a paragraph about how such wording should be legible and comprehensible to an average layperson reader who buys the product. Unfortunately, the *Miranda* statute contains no such statement about listener comprehensibility. Thus, the sequence of *Miranda* statements tends to be roughly the same as those noted earlier, summarized as follows:

1. Right to remain silent.
2. Statement may be held against you in court.

3. Right to have lawyer present.
4. Right to have lawyer appointed for you.
5. Right to terminate interview.

However good these statements are, their sequencing has a strange illogicality. The logic of the statement of rights indirectly suggests that the suspect first determine whether to remain silent by the end of Statement 1, *before* the right to have a lawyer present is suggested. If the issue of whether to have a lawyer present were suggested first, the decision whether to make statements might be resolved differently.

It is difficult to imagine how such a sequence was established and why lawyers have not challenged this issue. It is easy to see that clients do not realize that their first action is to be represented by a lawyer before considering their speaking/silence options.

Cohesiveness

The recitation of the arrest statement made by police to DWI suspects in my Dallas research shows that despite the logic in the arrest sequence, the lack of cohesion *within and between* sentences is sufficient to make them incomprehensible. The actual arrest statement used by the Dallas police is as follows:

(1) You are under arrest for the offense of driving while intoxicated.

(2) I request that you submit to taking a specimen of your breath for the purpose of analysis to determine the alcoholic content in your body.

(3) If you refuse to give a specimen, that refusal may be admissible in a subsequent prosecution.

(4) Your driver's license, permit or privilege to operate a motor vehicle will be automatically suspended for a period of 90 days after notice and hearing, if requested, whether or not you are prosecuted as a result of this arrest.

(5) If you do not possess this license to operate a motor vehicle, you may not be issued a license or permit to operate a motor vehicle for a period of 90 days after a notice and hearing if requested.

(6) Further, you have the right within 30 days after receiving a written notice of suspension or a denial, otherwise an R permit, to request in writing a hearing of the suspension or denial.

(7) If you provide the specimen I have requested, you then have the right to have your own physician draw a specimen of your blood within two hours of your arrest.

(8) Will you provide the specimen I have requested?

The DWI arrest statement sequence is progressively logical, but cohesion from sentence to sentence frequently fails. The relationship between (1) and (2), for example, is not specified; the listener must infer that the request is related to the arrest. A cohesion marker at the beginning of (2) would help, such as, "Because of this . . ." or "This causes me to request. . ."

Cohesion would be improved in (3) if "a specimen" were replaced with "this specimen." Even more preferable would be "this breath specimen" because *specimen* is more commonly understood to mean urine, bowel, or blood sample. Sentence (3) also introduces "in a subsequent prosecution" with no cohesive referent at all. This phrase is supposed to mean "in your possible prosecution," but the way it reads now implies the certainty of subsequent prosecution.

Sentence (4) could also be improved. The phrase "after notice and hearing, if requested" is introduced without cohesive markers. "If requested" remains ambiguous, but it appears that any possible hearing will occur only at the request of the subject. This ambiguity leads me to consider clarifying this sentence to read as follows:

> Your driver's license will be automatically suspended. After you have been given notice of your suspension, you have the right to request a hearing. Your suspension will be for a period of 90 days after you receive that notice or 90 days after the hearing if you choose to request one, whether or not you are prosecuted as a result of this arrest.

Although (5) and (6) have other minor cohesion problems, the next major problem is with (7). It specifies that the subject has the right to have his or her own physician draw a blood specimen from the subject but does not say why. It leaves the subject to infer that the physician-drawn blood sample will be used as a test of the accuracy of the breath sample taken by the police. This crucial point did not appear to be clear to the subjects.

Sentence Embedding and Complexity

Embedding results when clauses are joined or introduced by *and, but, or, when, if, so,* and *that.* Dallas officers introduce very little embedding into their own sentences; the major listener comprehension problem stems from the series of prepositional phrases found in the prescribed recitation. In the *Miranda* statement, a preposition occurs every 5.3 words. In the statement of arrest, a preposition occurs every 6.3 words. As a general principle, the more frequent the prepositions, the more embedded the language and the more difficult that language is to "decode."

Most listeners can process two or three levels of embedding without difficulty; the *Miranda* statement requires the listener to process embedding five to six layers deep, as follows:

1. You have the right
2. *to* have a lawyer present
3.   *to* advise you
4.   *prior to* or
5.   *during* any questioning.

1. If you are unable
2. *to* employ a lawyer, you have the right
3.   *to* have a lawyer appointed
4.   *to* advise you
5.   *prior to* and
6.   *during* questioning.

The deeper the embedding, the more apt the listener is to fail to comprehend.

In my study of suspect comprehension in DWI cases, I concluded that there are many reasons to believe that most suspects have serious difficulty understanding the statements of their rights. However appalled we may be at the horror and tragedy brought about by drunk drivers, the procedures used by law enforcement agencies in such cases should still be accurate, comprehensible, fair, and consistent. From what I observed, there are many reasons to believe that a suspect's comprehension does not always exist. Indications of failed comprehension include the following:

- ▶ Lack of clarity in the officers' reading of statements
- ▶ Lack of clarity in the statements themselves
- ▶ Requests for clarification
- ▶ Lack of effective response to requests for clarification
- ▶ Lack of concern for subject comprehension
- ▶ Use of terms of art, ambiguous language, or technical terminology or all three
- ▶ Use of indirect speech acts
- ▶ Lack of cohesion between and across sentences
- ▶ Lack of cohesion within sentences

► Use of complex or heavily embedded sentences or both

► Were the Rights of Jessie Moffett Abused?

The earliest police records of an investigation usually are memorialized in investigators' reports, summaries of what happened at a particular time. Such records are usually useful to the police as they leave a paper trail of their most significant, ongoing findings and document their procedures against any later challenges.

Detective R. A. Carey of San Diego Homicide Team 3 wrote up his report of his earliest contact with Jessie Moffett on April 13, 1979, some 24 hours after that contact. He reported the following:

On April 12, 1979, at 1208 hours, George SIMPSON, a secretary in Homicide, advised the undersigned officer that he had taken a telephone call from a man that would not give his name. SIMPSON related that the man wants to talk to the officer handling the 187 in Linda Vista. The man also told SIMPSON that he was in the park around 11:30 and he saw the victim alive, sitting up, with her left eye injured. He also realted [sic] that he had left his T-shirt with her. He then told SIMPSON that he would call back.

At 1220 hours, the undersigned officer received a telephone call from MOFFETT. He did not identify himself at this time. He related that he wanted to meet me at the L.V. Rec Center and we would go someplace to talk.

At 1300 hours, the undersigned officer interviewed Jesse MOFFETT in the parking lot of the Adoption Center, just east of the Linda Vista Recreation Center. Without taking notes, MOFFETT was asked to explain his situation. He immediately related that his main reason for meeting with the undersigned was to let him know that the fingerprints on the wall where we had dusted were probably his. He said he was in that area helping an injured girl on the night of the 10th. He went on to say that he was passing through the park, coming from his girlfriend's house and stopped at the Jack-in-the-Box on Fulton Street. He had passed the buildings, headed for his house, when he heard a female crying. He went in between the buildings and, where we had printed, he saw her kneeling down. He said he asked her what happened. She related to him that she didn't want anything to do with him and she tried to walk away from him. He said, [sic] at this time he pinned her against the wall because he wanted to help her. He said when he pinned her, he placed both hands up against the area where we had dusted for prints. He reiterated to her that he wanted to help her. He said at this time he could see she had a cut over her left eye and she was bleeding profusely. He then related that he asked her if she wanted him to call the police or if she wanted to go and call the police. Her answer to both of those questions was no.

He then told her his name and he believes she told him her name was Terri. He said she looked like she was under the influence of something. He asked her if it was alcohol and she said no. He asked her if it was LSD and she said no. When he asked her if she had been smoking weed, she did not answer.

During the time he contacted her, she kept coughing and spitting. While his white T-shirt was still on him, he attempted to pat the area that the blood was coming from. She then rubbed his T-shirt on her nose. At this time, he thought he might as well give it to her. He removed the T-shirt and placed it close to her injured eye. She held onto the T-shirt and the bleeding seemed to stop for awhile. At this time, he asked her who had hit her. She said it was her old man. He then asked her, "Your husband?" She nodded in the affirmative manner. At this time, she took the shirt away from her eye and the blood dripped down her face and onto her clothes. He reached up with his hands and touched the area. At this time, he wiped his bloody fingers on the wall of the restroom. He said this is probably where we got a bloody fingerprint. He said his palms may have been on there, also. He said he did this because he did not want to drip any blood on his pants.

The two of them then moved toward the auditorium door where the only lights for this area are located. He saw that she was a white female. It looked like she had somewhat of a tan on her face and arms. She was about 5'5" to 5'6", 120 to 125. He felt that she was between the age of 20 and 22 years. Her face was round. Her hair was brown and curly. It hung to her shoulders. Her eyebrows were real and she was kind of pretty, he said, because she looked natural. She was wearing a white blouse with green specks all through it. It was a short sleeve blouse. Her pants were brown or maroon. Her blouse was somewhat open and he could see that the blouse was kind of dirty because it looked brown. He could see that there was blood on her blouse.

He said at this location in front of the door she was bleeding once again. He grabbed her and he said he was very serious about helping her. He also said at this time that he would have beat up her old man if her old man would have shown up. When he grabbed her, she started screaming, "Leave me alone." At this time, he remembers telling her that he was going to leave. He said he left the area by going back through the two buildings where he had first seen her and out onto the grass area. When he reached the grass area, he looked behind him towards the entrance to the park. He saw a man walking toward the Recreation Center. He felt that he was white due to the fact that his hair was like a surfer's. He must have been about 6'1" and he weighted [*sic*] about 225 pounds, very wide shoulders. When he looked at this man, the man stopped waking [*sic*]. He said when he started up again, the man started walking towards the Recreation Center. He did not look back for about 2 minutes. It took him about 2 minutes to go down into the canyon area and up on top of the other side of the canyon. He turned then and he did not see anybody and did not hear anybody. He proceeded home and decided not to call the police.

He woke up the next morning around 10 and his mother told him that the police had surrounded the park and that there was a female dead. He wanted to call the police and let them know what he had done on that night, the night before, but his mother talked him out of it. She thought that he would probably get in trouble if he contacted the police. He finally decided on his own to contact the police because he wanted to let us know that his fingerprints were on the wall, but he was not responsible for her death.

He related that he had just got out of Tracy within the last month and that he had served time for purse snatch somewhere on Linda Vista Road. He related that on Monday he was going to work on Convoy Street. He gave the address 7771 Convoy Court. He related that he was willing to help us in any way in finding out who had killed the girl. I told him that I would contact him at his home concerning any future meetings.

The interview was terminated at 1400 hours.

The day following the first contact, on April 13, 3 hours before Detective Carey wrote his report on the April 12 meeting with Moffett, Carey had a second meeting with Moffett, which was memorialized in a second investigator's report that Carey wrote on April 16. The detective made it a point to indicate that he did not take notes during the first meeting on April 12, which resulted in a 3-page, single-spaced report. No mention was made of note taking in the second meeting on April 13, which resulted in a 1-page report. He emphasized in the second report that Moffett was advised of his constitutional rights. This report is as follows:

On 4-13-79, at 0915 hours, the undersigned officer contacted the witness by phone. A meeting was set up at the L.V. Recreation Center for 1045 hours. The undersigned proceeded to that location accompanied by Detective COX. The undersigned officer confronted the witness at 1100 hours. As we stood and talked by the auditorium the undersigned advised the witness of his constitutional rights. He said he understood his rights and then he wanted to know if he was going to be arrested. He was advised that he was not going to be arrested, but that it would be best if he was advised of his rights.

He related that instead of talking with me he would rather contact his Parole Officer and then he would see what would happen. Prior to leaving he asked me if we had any new evidence. He also asked me if we found any fingerprints between the walkway where he originally contacted the girl. I told him that we did have good prints off of the walls.

He then advised the undersigned that that [sic] last he saw of her was right where we were standing. He said he left her here with his t-shirt and walked through the buildings pointing to where he first contacted her. He was asked if he had ever gone down the walk that night with her toward the handball courts. He said he never has been down there because he's only been in the park twice since he got out of Tracy. He also stated he did not see a radio or a bronze colored jacket.

Prior to leaving the presence of the undersigned he said some of the guys in the area had told him that some lunatic that lives in the area did it. He said he knew his name.

The undersigned advised him that he didn't have to tell but it would be in his best interest and the communities [*sic*] interest that he devulge [*sic*] the name. He did not give the undersigned the lunatic's name. He then said that he would call me in about an hour if got ahold of his Parole Agent to discuss a new meeting.

The interview was terminated at 1110 hours.

If a tape recording had been made of this conversation, it might have sounded like this.

Detective: Do you understand your rights?

Witness: Yeah, but am I gonna be arrested?

Detective: No, but it's best that you be advised of your rights.

Witness: I'd rather talk to my parole officer first and then see what's gonna happen. Do you have any new evidence?

Detective: [no response]

Witness: Did you find any fingerprints between the walkway where I seen the lady?

Detective: Yes, we have good prints off the walls.

Witness: Well, the last I seen her was right here where we standin'. I left her here with my T-shirt and walked through them buildings.

Detective: Did you go down the walk with her toward the handball courts?

Witness: I never been down there. I only been in the park twice since I got out of Tracy.

Detective: Did you see a radio there?

Witness: No.

Detective: Did you see a bronze-colored jacket?

Witness: No.

Detective: Who did it?

Witness: Some guys in this area told me that some lunatic that lives around here did it.

Detective: Do you know his name?

Witness: Yeah.

Detective: You don't have to tell me that man's name, but it would be in your best interest to tell me who it is.

Witness: No, I ain't gonna do that.

Detective: OK. You're gonna call me then after you talk to your parole agent?

Witness: Yeah, I'll call you.

Curiously enough, on April 30, 1979, Detective Carey produced a second investigator's report of the same meeting with Moffett on April 13 at the recreation center. It is as follows:

On April 13, 1979, at 1100 hours, the undersigned met with Jesse MOFFETT at the Linda Vista Rec Center. The meeting had been prearanged [sic]. The undersigned advised MOFFETT that he wanted MOFFETT to go over the story he had told on the previous day concerning his contact with the white female on the night of the 10th. He was also advised that his rights would have to be read to him. The undersigned advised him of his constitutional rights per PD-4115.

His first question was "am I going to be busted?" He was advised that he was not, he was advised that it was a necessity for the undersigned to advise him of his constitutional rights due to his involvement.

He then related that he wanted to talk to his parole agent and would like his parole agent present. He said he would go home and contact his parole agent by phone and then call the undersigned. Prior to leaving the undersigned's presence he said that the area where we were standing was where he could see her clear because of the lights. At this time we were right under the two lights that are over the door to the auditorium.

He was asked if he was north of this location at any time with the female. He said he was never north down the walkway toward Genesee. He said he hasn't been in that part of the Rec since he's been out of prison. He went on to relate that he did not see a radio or the bronze jacket the victim had left behind. He also said that some lunatic did it but he did not and that he had gained that information from some other people in the park. He did not give the undersigned a name. He then reiterated that he would contact the undersigned officer after he contacted his parole agent. He was asked who his parole agent was and he said I think his name is SNOWDEN. It was later found that his parole agent was SNEDDEN.

Interview terminated at 1110 hours.

This report raises an interesting *Miranda* issue. After having been read his rights, Moffett said he wanted to talk to his parole agent and would like to have this person present at any questioning. Notice that, on April 16, Officer

Carey reports that the next thing Moffett said was that the area where he was standing was where he could see the young lady because of the lights. But on April 30, Detective Carey reports that the next thing Moffett asked was whether there was any new evidence and whether the police found any fingerprints. By the time Detective Carey appeared at a hearing in this case, some 11 years later, he had no memory of even having written the two reports. In any case, the issue was not that Carey reported somewhat different things in the two reports as much as it was why he continued to ask Moffett questions after the suspect had not waived his rights.

In Detective Carey's April 30 report of the incident, he notes that he then asked Moffett a question. If a tape recording had been made of this conversation, it might have sounded like this:

Detective: Were you north of here at any time with the female?

Witness: I was never north of the walkway toward Genesee. I ain't been in that part of the Rec since I got out of prison.

Detective: Did you see a radio there?

Witness: No.

Detective: Did you see a bronze jacket that the lady left behind?

Witness: No.

Detective: Well, who do you think did it?

Witness: Some people say it was probably some lunatic.

Detective: What's his name?

Witness: I ain't gonna tell you 'til I talk to my parole agent. I'll call you after that.

Detective: Who is your parole agent?

Witness: I think it Snoden.

Although we don't have a tape recording to verify that the above interaction took place, Detective Carey's reports provide enough information to indicate clearly that after Moffett refused to waive his rights, the questioning continued. At a hearing in the Superior Court of the State of California, San Diego, on August 21, 1989, Carey argued that Moffett continued to volunteer information after he refused to waive, as follows:

A: I'm sure we didn't talk to him at all after advising him of his rights. He immediately wanted his, to talk to his parole agent.

Q: You did continue to have a conversation with him about certain items, though. Is that right?

A: He continued conversation after he wanted his parole agent, then he started relating to where he saw the lady at the scene on his own.

Q: Right.

A: So we went ahead and asked a few questions, such as, "Were you down at the lower section of the park at that time?" To which he said, "No."

Later at this same hearing, Detective Carey reiterated that Moffett volunteered information after refusing waiver:

Q: Did you question him anymore at that point?

A: Yes, we did.

Q: What led up to that?

A: He volunteered information concerning his night with the young lady at the scene.

Q: He volunteered? That was not in response to some further questions by you?

A: That's correct.

Q: And what did he volunteer to you?

A: He volunteered that this was the area, pointing at where he first saw the young lady. And then after explaining to us certain things, he, we then asked him, "Well, were you down in the lower section of the park?" and he said, "No."

At issue here, as far as *Miranda* rights are concerned, is whether the interrogation of Moffett should have stopped after he refused to waive his rights. An actual tape recording of this interrogation would have resolved the issue one way or the other. Unfortunately, although the police recorded many other things in this case, they did not record this event. Thus, we are left with only the investigator's two reports of the same incident, written 2 weeks apart, and with his fragile memory of the event some 10 years later. As it turns out, Carey's memory depended almost entirely on his reference to the reports, as the transcript of his testimony continuously reveals. But even using only the available evidence and not resorting to the reconstructions suggested earlier, Carey's reports indicate clearly that Moffett was asked questions after he refused to waive his rights, as the following reveal:

April 16, 1979, Investigator's Report

1. "*He was asked* if he had ever gone down the wall that night with her toward the handball courts."
2. "The undersigned *advised him that he didn't have to tell* but it would be in his best interest and the communities [*sic*] interest that he devulge [*sic*] the name."

April 30 Investigator's Report

3. "*He was asked* if he was north of this location at any time with the female."
4. "He went on to relate that he did not see a radio or a bronze jacket the victim had left behind."
5. "He also said that some lunatic did it"
6. "he had gained that information from some other people in the park"
7. "He would not give the undersigned a name."
8. "*He was asked* who his parole agent was."

There can be no question about (1) above. Carey flatly states that Moffett was *asked*. Although (2) is not in the form of a question (ending with a question mark), it implies a question inasmuch as any listener, upon hearing this, would naturally feel the need to agree or disagree in order to continue the conversation. Linguists have demonstrated how many utterances that have the form of a statement clearly carry the function of a question. For example, "Tell me everything you know about the event," though a directive in form, clearly operates as a question. Evidence of this can be found in the response, which indicates that the listener understood the alleged directive to actually be a request, or question.

Likewise, in his April 30 investigator's report, Carey admits to asking a question in (3) and (8). And (4) is a fascinating example in that it must be understood in the light of the *given-new principle* in discourse analysis. This principle states that any information discussed can be categorized as either old (given) or new; contextual variables make clear which category obtains. In an investigator's report of this type, many of the contextual clues that would be accessible in a tape-recorded conversation are inaccessible. But one important contextual clue remains: If Moffett had brought up the subject of a radio or bronze jacket left behind by the victim, this would indicate that he knew considerably more about the murder than he otherwise admitted. Obviously, the radio and the jacket were important clues, and only the police could have brought up this topic. The only question that remains, then, is how the police brought up this topic. It is difficult to imagine any way for them to have introduced important evidence not mentioned by the suspect other than by means of a question.

To a slightly lesser extent, the same could be said of (5). Why would Moffett volunteer that bystanders said a lunatic did it? The police would say that he did so to throw suspicion off himself. But if this were the case, why wouldn't Moffett tell them whom *he* thought the killer was, rather than attribute this to bystanders?

In the list above, (6) either is Moffett's response to a follow-up question to his previous answer that a lunatic did it ("Who told you that?") or was embedded in Moffett's original response to the question "Who did it?" In addition, (7) is clearly Moffett's response to a follow-up question to his answer that bystanders said it was a lunatic.

The issue here is whether Jessie Moffett's rights were violated when the investigators continued to ask him questions after he refused to waive his rights. The court was faced with the choice of either believing Detective Carey's assertion that Moffett "volunteered" information after he requested counsel or analyzing what was said in the two police reports, along with Detective Carey's statements at the hearing.

It is difficult to disbelieve law enforcement officers, especially when the defendant's reputation is not sterling. Nor is the account presented here intended to indicate that the police were lying; they may well have been convinced that Moffett had actually volunteered further information without being questioned. But two factors argue that Moffett's rights had, indeed, been violated. The first factor is that virtually every other encounter that Moffett had with the police was tape-recorded. For some unknown reason, however, there is no tape recording of this crucial event. The second and more crucial factor is that the language in Detective Carey's two written police reports offers clear evidence that Moffett was questioned after he refused to waive his rights. It is difficult to imagine how Detective Carey's explicit statements that Moffett "was asked" could be understood in any other way but that the detective asked and Moffett answered. Had the court been trained linguistically or permitted linguistic testimony about the given-new principle, it might well have been inclined to view the matter differently. Perhaps the use of linguistic expertise in the area of law is still too new for some courts, but the Moffett case clearly points to its usefulness.

Whereas police inspectors are permitted to accuse, lie, flatter, talk roughly, trick, and play act during the interrogation itself, the presentation of a suspect's rights permits no such tactics. The interrogation must be free of evidence of coercion or trickery. Nearly five pages of the *Miranda* act are highly critical of techniques that stress the need for the interrogator to present a false persona to the subject, pretend to sympathize with him or her, present fake or misleading interpretation of events, or give erroneous legal advice. Even the conventional good guy-bad guy interrogation routine comes under criticism in matters of presenting *Miranda* rights.

An interesting issue arises when a suspect is being interrogated before his or her constitutional rights are read. In Jessie Moffett's case, his attorney, Geraldine Russell, contended that during the totality of the circumstances surrounding his repeated interrogations, the conduct of the police constituted deception when they concealed from Moffett their motivation for questioning him. Russell contended that by not telling Moffett what charges they were contemplating for him, they were, in effect, deliberately misleading him and concealing their intent. At one point in the April 17, 1979, interrogation, the following exchange took place:

Detective: Where does he come in on this, after the incident, did you confide in him the next day, or was he there with you that night, or what?

Witness: Well, I'd just rather hold that off.

Detective: Well, that may save a lot of problems for you.

Witness: What do you mean by problems?

Detective: Just what I said, problems.

Witness: So what kind of problems do I have?

Detective: I don't know. We're still investigating this right now to this minute. I don't know what's going to happen in the next minute or two along this investigation. We just gotta keep talking to people.

It is clear that, in this exchange, Moffett was requesting information about his status and what types of charges the police were contemplating. But the detective avoids stating that Moffett faces the accusation of murder or that the police actually consider him a suspect. Defense Attorney Russell claimed that by failing to notify Moffett that he was a suspect and by presenting the false facade that they were merely trying to gather information or, even worse, that they were trying to clear his name, the police denied Moffett an effective warning that a crucial stage of the adversarial process had begun. One desired result of *Miranda* is that the warning will make persons acutely aware that they are faced with a phase of the adversarial system. When the accused are kept from such knowledge through deception, the desired effect of the warning is lost and the suspects are denied their opportunity to make a knowing and intelligent waiver of their rights. Moffett was tried and convicted of first-degree murder. Although linguistic analysis was provided to his defense, no resources were made available to facilitate such testimony at trial.

► **Were the Rights of Charles Lorraine Violated?**

In May 1986, an elderly woman was brutally murdered in her Warren, Ohio, home, stabbed to death with a pair of scissors in what appeared to be a robbery. For various reasons, a young man named Charles Lorraine was brought in by the police as a prime suspect. The police videotaped his confession, and he was indicted and brought to trial. The state assigned him a public defender, Michael Gleespen, who subsequently contacted me to assess the confession tape. In his confession, Lorraine clearly admitted to the brutal murder, but the public defender had considerable doubts about Lorraine's waiver of his rights.

The prosecution claimed that a certain portion of the tape that preceded Lorraine's confession read as follows:

18:59 p.m.

Detective Seese: It ain't gonna go away, Chuck. It's gonna stay there.

Detective Andrews: It's gonna be here today, tomorrow, the next day.

Lorraine: Can't you shut the tape off?

Detective Andrews: We need it on, Charles. For your benefit as well as ours.

Lorraine: I, I don't want to talk.

Detective Andrews: You don't want to talk?

Detective Seese: If we shut it off? If we turn the tape off, will you tell us?

19:00 p.m.

Lorraine: I, I'd wanna talk. Turn the tape off.

Detective Andrews: OK.

Detective Seese: OK.

Lorraine: And the TV.

Detective Seese: All right.

Officer Teeple: [running the video recorder/camera] You want it off or on?

Unknown: [syllable, as if word cut off]
[video turned off for 15 minutes]

19:15 p.m.

Lorraine: Me and Perry went, we broke the window first at the lady's house. After we broke the window, we ran to the Olympic, we went up to, ah, we went, er, ah, Victor's. Went up there, smoked a couple joints . . .

Obviously, the police believed that after Lorraine asked that the tape be shut off and after he said that he didn't want to talk, he then changed his mind and agreed to talk with no recording being done. Thus, they shut off the video recorder while Lorraine confessed to everything.

Public Defender Gleespen was unsure, however, about exactly what Lorraine said at 19:00. It didn't sound like "I'd wanna talk" to him, but he couldn't tell exactly what was said. He sent me the tape, and I concluded that what the police believed to be "I, I'd wanna talk" was actually the exact opposite, "Look, I, I don't wanna talk."

In my testimony at trial, I presented four aspects of linguistic analysis supporting my finding that Lorraine was saying that he did not want to talk further. On the whole, the defense transcript was much the same as the prosecution's. The major difference was where the prosecution transcript indicates that Lorraine said, "I, I'd wanna talk." After many careful listenings to these words, I produced four linguistic analyses that support the defense version:

1. The negative meaning of *look*
2. The phonetic reduction of *don't*
3. The number of syllables used
4. The intonation used

The Negative Meaning of *Look*

The statement is uttered quickly and with heightened emotion. It begins with the word *look*. This sentence beginner is significant in English at such a juncture in the conversation because it signals disagreement with what was said by the immediately preceding speaker. Many examples of such disagreement can be cited in English, but the following hypothetical example will suffice:

Husband: I'd like beef for dinner tonight.
Wife: Look, I told you we don't have any beef.

The semantics of *look* in such a sentence is the same semantics found in Lorraine's statement. It can be glossed as "I already told you," "Can't you understand what I'm saying?" or in other similar ways to indicate disagreement, if not frustration.

The Phonetic Reduction of *Don't*

Emotionally charged speech is often spoken quickly, and in his statement, Lorraine speaks very rapidly. In rapid speech, *phonetic reductions* occur. Nasal consonants (e.g., *n, m*) in word-final position are often the first to be reduced. The word *don't,* for example, is regularly reduced from /dont/ to /don/ (reducing or deleting the *t*) and even more to "duh"; that is, the final *t* and the semifinal *n* are deleted, or reduced, leaving only the initial *d* followed by the schwa vowel /uh/. Such reduction is common in the rapid speech of most native speakers of English, but only when the word that follows *don't* begins with a consonant sound, including the *w* sound of *wanna*.

The Number of Syllables Used

Close listening to this statement indicates that Lorraine did indeed produce "duh" in this utterance. To check this further, I played the utterance on my Marantz PMD 200 tape recorder, which has a variable speed control that can slow the speech as much as 15%. Slowing Lorraine's utterance verified a "duh" sequence, and the syllabicity of this utterance was as follows (each dash indicates the presence of one syllable):

___, _, _ __ ____ _ __.
Look, I, I duh wann- a talk.

If Lorraine had said, "Look, I, I wanna talk," the syllabicity would have had a different configuration as follows:

———, —' — ——— — ——.
Look, I, I wann- a talk.

Of crucial interest here is that Lorraine produced seven syllables, not six. Seven syllables are one too many for the utterance to be considered an agreement to talk.

The Intonation Used

Intonation is the combined pitch level and stress (sometimes called *accent*) patterns of language. *Pitch* ranges from high to low; *stress* ranges from loud to soft. In English, high pitch accompanies loud stress. One way to represent intonation is by accompanying the words used with lines of three different heights: a high line for high intonation, a mid line for middle intonation, and a low line for low intonation. In this utterance, Lorraine uses only mid and high intonation. Lorraine's statement is thus represented as follows:

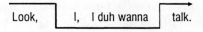

Such an intonation pattern is consistent with an objection, with negativity, and it is not consistent with agreement or positivity. Had Lorraine attempted to use positive, agreement intonation, the levels would have been as follows:

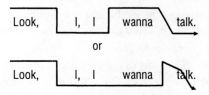

The major difference between the actual intonation pattern used by Lorraine and Pattern A above is that the latter shows stress and high pitch on *wanna,* with sentence falling pitch on *talk.* In the speech actually used by Lorraine, the word-final intonation remains at a high level and does not fall. The same falling intonation sets off Pattern B from Lorraine's actual speech.

It is clear from Lorraine's intonation, then, that his utterance was one of objection, not agreement.

These four aspects of Lorraine's actual speech (the negative sentence introducer, his phonetic reduction of *n* in *don't,* his use of seven syllables that verifies negation, and his intonation of objection) all converge and combine to provide evidence from his own speech patterns that he was, indeed, saying that he did not want to talk.

In a hearing at the end of July 1986, my findings were presented in court, and the judge ruled that the government's interpretation, rather than mine, was correct. Perhaps my analysis was too esoteric for the judge. But this is not the only judge to state that his own hearing is superior to that of the expert witness linguist.

The Future of *Miranda*

The government has made considerable progress in recent years to ensure that suspects are fully aware of their rights when they are brought before law enforcement officers. This is not to say, however, that *Miranda* is secure. Legal scholars, such as Joseph Grano (1993), are arguing that *Miranda* should be overturned. Grano claims that even though most suspects are not on equal footing with their interrogators at the police station, such inequality should be of "no concern" because it would "thwart the search for truth because *guilty defendants* [italics added] who are an equal match for their interrogators will know that it is generally not in their interest to cooperate" (p. 34). Grano also rejects the argument that most suspects are from poor and uneducated portions of the population, dismissing the egalitarianism argument as "a powerful tug on the emotions" (p. 35). Such anti-*Miranda* sentiment also argues that police interrogations are not coercive. Grano observes, "that police sometimes seriously misbehave lends no support to the view that police efforts at persuasion must be viewed as coercive" (p. 54). The difference between fact finding and persuasion is blurred in such thinking. Grano argues that it is not cruel to force those who are innocent to run the gauntlet of adversarial cross-examination because the police cannot be certain about guilt or innocence and the police are acting in good faith (p. 55).

Others argue that the problem is not so much with the *Miranda* law as it is with the way *Miranda* is implemented. The three situations and cases described in this chapter point to weaknesses in such implementation and describe how linguistic analysis can be used to challenge it.

▶ Notes

1. For an excellent discussion of confession law, see Inbau et al., 1986; and Nissman et al., 1985.

2. A version of this section appeared originally in *The Champion,* May 1987, pp. 23-46.

Language of Truthfulness and Deception

4

n their excellent book *Deceptive Communication,* Miller and Stiff (1993) review the state of research on the topic of deception. They point out that most of this research has been on detecting deception by means of nonverbal clues (p. 21). But even when research subjects are able to identify verbal content accurately, they rely almost exclusively on nonverbal behavior to make judgments about deception (p. 46). Because the pioneers of deception research were mostly physiologists and social psychologists, it is only natural that such work would focus on physiological features that accompany deceptive behavior, rather than on language itself. Thus, the polygraph had its moment in the sun before falling out of favor, succeeded by nonverbal behavior that, using Ekman's (1984) term, "leaked" during deception. Various indicators, however, such as nervousness and twitching, were immediately problematic because nervous behavior is present in deception but is not equivalent to deceptive behavior. By the mid-1980s, paralinguistic features were investigated as well, including length of pauses, length of responses, speech errors, and specificity of references (Cody, Marston, & Foster, 1984). Although the latter work comes closer to the study of verbal language and offers promise for future study, the results of research so far offer conflicting conclusions. The most consistent correlates of deception have been that deceivers give shorter answers than truthful speakers and that deceivers are less specific and more overgeneralized (using more "allness" terms such as *every, none, all, always*).

Miller and Stiff (1993) point out a serious weakness in the research on deception carried out to date: "Many researchers have investigated either correlates of actual deception or correlates of deception detection accuracy, but few have integrated these two research traditions" (p. 65). That is, findings indicate what clues the research subjects claim they relied on with some consistency, but these clues did not strongly correlate with the actual statements that were judged. This weakness led Miller and Stiff to conclude that the clues that observers *claim* to rely on to make judgments about truth and deception are, on the whole, not really related to actual honesty or deceit.

Robinson (1996) provides a comprehensive review of theory and research on lying and deceit, noting how different academic fields differ in their approaches to this phenomenon. Especially relevant to the focus of this book is Robinson's Chapters 3 and 4, "Lying Face to Face: Standing Features" and "Lying Face to Face: General Dynamics," in which he reviews the work of many scholars, most notably that of Ekman (1985) and Miller and Stiff (1993). Robinson's conclusions, like those of Ekman and Miller and Stiff, are not optimistic about the ability of humans to detect lying and deceit. In fact, accuracy of the detection of deceitful language is, according to the research reported by Miller and Stiff, at about the level of chance:

> Krant and Poe (1980) found that customs inspectors were equally inaccurate in their judgments of deception as laypeople. Recently, Ekman and O'Sullivan (1991) reported that several occupational groups, including federal polygraphers, robbery investigators, judges, and psychiatrists, were not significantly more accurate at detecting deception than college students . . . humans are poor lie detectors. (p. 69)

Miller and Stiff (1993) point out five problems with the research based on deceptive communication:

1. Such studies do not assess the accuracy of detection but simply point out differences in the accuracy of deception between different experimental conditions (p. 70).
2. After years of finding low accuracy rates on subjects' abilities to detect deception, the research continues as though it were successful, whereas a radical change in approach is indicated (p. 71).
3. Research on deception is based on experiments that do not reflect real life adequately. In most of life, we do not get the chance to choose between an equal number of true and deceptive statements to make our judgments of veracity. To be sure, most of us are lied to, but not on a 50-50 basis, probably not even on the basis of 1 statement out of 20. When subjects in an experiment are conditioned to believe that each statement to be judged is either false or true, the likelihood of making a judgment of deception increases greatly, whether accurate or not.

4. When nonverbal or verbal clues to veracity are used, one first needs a baseline of information about the speaker being judged. Some people are often more nervous than others. Some eye-blink more frequently than others. In some cultures, pausing and eye-avoidance are more natural than in others.

5. Deception research often overlooks the role of the interrogator's language in the suspect's response. A question asked with skepticism tends to increase eye-blinks, hand gestures, and response length more than probes that convey to subjects that the interviewer believes them (p. 91).

To Miller and Stiff's list, the linguist might add one important problem with the previous research: It follows the paradigm of psychology in that it is experimental in structure. Such a methodology has the advantage of controlling the variables, but it also has some disadvantages. One disadvantage is that this research protocol is not the actual event; it is, at best, a re-creation of the actual or potential event, craftily constructed to emulate reality. In some ways it succeeds, much as a female impersonator succeeds in making nightclub patrons believe he is a woman, or political cartoons succeed in making readers believe they are seeing the actual object of the artist's pen. One outgrowth of experimental control is the compression of reality into smaller units that focus on the issue being studied. A concomitant disadvantage of such compression is the elimination of recurring instances that actual life provides. Such recurrence offers the best language indicator of deceptive language: inconsistency. People get caught when they tell different facts at different times. To obtain such inconsistency, however, one needs a longer research protocol than most experiments will permit. Furthermore, keeping track of inconsistencies is not an easy thing to do because language goes by us very quickly and our own conversational agendas tend to prevent us from keeping tabs on the agendas of our conversational partners.

Programs have been offered to law enforcement agencies to help their personnel determine whether a suspect is being deceitful. Features of subject behavior covered often include nonverbal clues, in addition to verbal clues such as the following:

► Providing overly detailed statements
► Repeating oneself spontaneously
► Complicating the story unexpectedly
► Giving unusual details
► Providing marginally relevant details
► Giving related external associations

- ▶ Displaying subjectivity
- ▶ Correcting spontaneously
- ▶ Admitting memory loss
- ▶ Hedging
- ▶ Self-referencing excessively
- ▶ Manifesting verbosity
- ▶ Pausing excessively
- ▶ Using unnecessary connectors
- ▶ Using pronoun deviations such as *you* for *I*
- ▶ Producing disproportionate amounts of language in the prologue, central action, or epilogue portions of the narrative
- ▶ Producing low lexical diversity by means of type-token ratio

Developers of the police training programs claim that these features of verbal language, working together in some unspecified combination, will let the interrogating officers know how truthful or deceitful suspects are.

Because of the paucity of research evidence about the usefulness of these or any other verbal clues in determining deceit, Porter and Yuille (1996) performed a fascinating study in which university students were told that a plainclothes security officer had been hired to combat a recent rash of thefts at the school. The scenario was that these students were to be used as a test of the officer's ability to discover whether suspects were telling the truth. In actuality, Porter and Yuille wanted to know whether the major verbal clues presented by training programs to law enforcement officers (listed above) were valid and accurate indicators of deceit. They took these 17 verbal indicators from the following police training programs:

- ▶ *Statement Validity Analysis,* widely used in child abuse investigations in Germany (Undeutsch, 1982), includes a validity checklist of individual characteristics and motivations of a subject and criteria-based content analysis that deals with verbal aspects, such as the high degree of detail that characterizes credible speech (Steller & Koehnken, 1989).
- ▶ *Reality Monitoring* (Leippe, Manion, & Romandzyk, 1992) suggests that true memories yield greater sensory information, whereas created memories use more internally created details and subjective information (Johnson & Raye, 1981).
- ▶ Sapir's SCAN *Training Program* avers, among other things, that deceivers use lengthier introductions, unnecessary connectors, and important pronoun deviations (Sapir, 1987).

► *Lexical Diversity* (Hollien, 1990) argues that suspects trying to appear truthful display low lexical diversity by means of type-token ratio because language behavior under increased drive becomes stereotypical (Osgood, 1960).

Different tasks were assigned to different groups of students, some to "steal" money from a locked office, others to carry out the legitimate task of "retrieving" a folder from a locked office. They were then to test the ability of the interviewer to determine whether they were lying about what they did. One group was to confess the truth, one was to create a truthful alibi, one was to deceive partially, and one was to invent a false alibi. The subjects were all motivated by a payment for their work. The interview itself was conducted by "officers" trained in the stepwise interview (Yuille, Hunter, Joffe, & Zaparniuk 1993), which moves logically and effectively from open-ended questions to general and then specific ones.

Through multivariate analysis, only 3 of the 18 language features showed any significance. Truthful subjects produced more details, were twice as coherent, and admitted memory loss more often. The three significant language features were all taken from statement analysis (criteria-based content analysis). Lest this program be given too much credibility, however, it should be pointed out that seven of the statement analysis verbal features did not reach the level of significance. None of the other verbal features, all from Sapir's SCAN, the Reality Monitoring, and the Type-Token Analysis programs, displayed any significance.

Research that is conducted in laboratory settings, as opposed to real-life events, will always raise questions. This research also has other debatable aspects, as the researchers themselves point out. But their results must be seriously considered by the law enforcement agencies that have been using approaches such as these. As much as it is attractive to believe that specific language features associate with deceit, there is simply not enough proof of this to justify using them.

I have been asked many times, often by zealous prosecutors, whether I can tell if a speaker is lying. I answer, quite candidly, that I cannot. But most liars are not good at prevarication, especially during complex and pressure-packed interrogation by law enforcement officers. They tend to slip up somewhere and become inconsistent. When they do, they can get caught in their inconsistent language.

Ekman (1985) points out two ways to lie: (a) through outright falsification and (b) through concealment. Inconsistency is one signal that either approach is untruthful. Linguistic science cannot penetrate the inner motives and thoughts of the human mind, but when the language used by a person becomes the evidence against him or her, it is possible to check that language for inconsistencies. A linguist can point out, through analytical categories and approaches that would not normally occur to a juror or even to a prosecutor, when the speaker is consistent or inconsistent.

▶ Was Robert Alben Lying?

Such a situation presented itself in the case of Robert Alben (not his real name), a native New Yorker transplanted to Florida, whose wife was brutally murdered in January 1977. Her husband was one of several suspects in the case, and he was interrogated by the police the next day. For whatever reasons, charges were not brought against Alben until 1990, when the prosecutor again considered indicting him for the murder of his wife.

The major evidence against Alben in this case was his confession statement made to the police on January 26, 1977. Knowing of my interest and experience in confession cases, Alben's attorney, Lyle Bruce, asked me to examine the tape-recorded statement and to prepare to be an expert witness at Alben's trial.

In his statement, Alben states over and over again that he does not remember anything during the block of time in which his wife was attacked. He says he has a problem when he has had several alcoholic drinks, causing him to black out or sleep deeply. He recalls events up to a certain point on the day of his wife's murder and the day after it, but nothing at the crucial time frame signaled by the police. The question asked by all, of course, was whether this memory loss, blackout, or whatever else was an evasive concealment or the truth.

One of the first things that struck me about this "confession" statement was that Alben openly admitted to continuous and recent arguments with his wife, including an argument the evening before her murder. He even admitted to having slapped her during an argument a week earlier. He admits that their relationship was strained and that he has a bad temper. It is common for liars to deny the conditions that lead up to the crime for which they are charged, along with the crime itself, as a way of avoiding suspicion. But Alben didn't do this. Was he then telling the truth? Or was he just a highly skilled liar throwing a smoke screen to confuse the issue? If it was an intentional smoke screen, it was a very dangerous one because it provided the police with a motive for the murder. If it was a maneuver on Alben's part, it was a gamble of the first order, one that might befit a professional con man, such as Mel Weinberg of the FBI's Abscam investigation in the early 1980s. Alben gave no other evidence of being a con artist who could carry off a gamble that, by providing the police with his possible motive, would convince them he was telling the truth about his drunken blackout at the time of the murder. Although this was by no means perfect evidence that Alben was telling the police the truth, it was enough to cause me to examine whether his story was consistent elsewhere.

As Bruce and I thought about how to present Alben's case to a jury, it occurred to me that we might start with Alben's admissions of arguing with his wife. The linguistic analytical routine would be speech act analysis, in this case the speech act of admitting. Bruce would ask me, "Dr. Shuy, what does Alben admit in his statement to the police?" My response would be to produce a chart of all the things our client admitted, as follows:

- ► Arguing with his wife
- ► Drinking problem
- ► Has a temper
- ► Unreported income

As far as this case was concerned, Alben's admissions about past arguments with his wife were central:

Alben Admits Arguing With His Wife

Tape A	6:10	I had an argument with my wife because a waitress said I looked familiar. She made a remark. I frequently go there because I want to open a restaurant with that place. My wife thought I was having an affair.
Tape B	3:53	I've argued with her for months—her medical condition. She argues with everyone.
	Q:	So your relationship has been strained?
	A:	It has been strained. That's why I pleaded with her to go away for the weekend . . . get away together.
Tape B	5:09	She takes medication hormones or something. If she doesn't take it, she goes berserk. The doctor said don't take it, it's cancerous. She pleaded with the doctor to let her take it. He agreed to let her take one every other day. I pleaded with her to go to a gynecologist. Instead of a gynecologist, she went to a diet doctor to pop pills. Her mother and I started screaming at her—take care of your health.

Tape C	0:15	Q:	Did you ever strike her?
		A:	Last week, the first time in 29 years . . . I slapped her when she told her mother over the phone I was beating her up. I took the phone from her, hung it up, and slapped her across the face. Her mother came over and said you've not been touched. She gets black and blue.
Tape C	2:51		She's been driving me crazy for months. Her mother also.

What is significant about his chart, of course, is that it does not contain any admission that Alben killed his wife. One reason for taking this approach was to defuse what might be considered the worst part of Alben's statement by focusing on what it does not say. After all, the prosecution considered the statement a confession. The defense thought otherwise. If the worst they could find was a potential motive for killing his wife, we would start with this and construct our case in such a way as to make the idea seem frivolous. After all, many marriages are strained, and many middle-aged women have similar reactions to hormone medication and irritate their family.

The next question my analysis was to address was the head-on issue, Did Alben admit to attacking his wife? My answer to that, still part of my speech act analysis, was a chart citing all the statements by Alben in which he did not admit this, as follows:

Alben Does Not Admit to Killing His Wife

Tape B	3:00	Q:	Did you do it?
		A:	I don't think I did. It's not in me to do it. If I can't kill an animal, can't kill a dog, why would I want to do something like this?
Tape B	3:20	Q:	Why would you want to do something like this?
		A:	Why? Lived with a woman for 29 years, I want to kill her? . . . I don't want to kill my wife. I'm praying that she gets better up there.
Tape B	12:12	Q:	Are you telling us the truth?
		A:	As God is my witness, I am.
Tape B	15:34	Q:	Did you strike your wife with a hammer?
		A:	Honestly, I don't think so. I pray to God I didn't. I don't remember, I swear to God. You have to be honest with me. You have ways of finding out. You have to know. You're conning me now. . . . I stood there and looked at her. She can't talk. I want to ask her, did I do it? Don't you understand? . . . No, you don't understand. You're not in my place. You're sitting over there.

Tape C	3:32	Q:	You think she drove you to do this?
		A:	No, I could take my clothes and move out. I wouldn't do this to her.
Tape C	7:07		I bought her a diamond necklace. Do you buy a necklace for your wife if you're going to kill her? . . . I don't think I'm the guy that does a thing like that. I don't do that.

The interrogator's five questions here all fall within the prescribed limits of police interrogation. The first is direct and forthright: "Did you do it?" The second approaches the issue from Alben's motivation and presupposes that he actually did the deed. The third challenges Alben's truthfulness. Although it also accuses Alben of doing it, such accusation is legally acceptable in police interrogations. The fourth is direct and straightforward, adding the alleged murder weapon. The last question is a classic in interrogations of this type, again presupposing that Alben actually did the deed but offering him a somewhat sympathetic motive.

Alben's responses may seem a bit odd to those unfamiliar with New York Jewish conversational style. Alben was a New Yorker who had moved to Florida fairly recently, and the style of answering a question with another question was quite natural for him.

What is missing from these non-admissions of guilt, of course, is Alben's speech act of denying. He does not admit attacking his wife, but he does not deny it either. This, of course, was the next question that Bruce would ask me: "I note that the title of your chart here does *not* say, 'Alben Denies Attacking His Wife.' Why is this?" My answer was that Alben couldn't deny it simply because he says he cannot remember doing it. I then cited all the instances in which Alben said he cannot remember attacking his wife:

Alben Cannot Remember Hitting His Wife

Tape A	10:31	I can't tell you. I wish I did know. I want you to tell me if you know.
Tape A	12:42	I'm trying to be honest with you. I don't know. If I don't know, I don't know.
Tape A	14:30	I wish I did remember what happened after I left the track. I wish I did.

Tape A	18:14		That's all I remember. I swear to God, I don't remember.
Tape B	2:08		Talk to me. Tell me something, please. I have nothing else to say to you. Talk to me. I'm pleading with you now. I'm looking at you, please. Be honest with me. You have my fingerprints. If I did this goddamn thing, for God's sakes tell me. I can't, you've got to be honest with me. I want to know. You're looking at me like, what's the matter, talk to me.
Tape B	13:12		I blame myself because I don't know what happened, don't you understand?
Tape B	15:34		I don't remember, I swear to God.
Tape C	0:10	Q:	You think you could've had just too much, and hit her?
		A:	I don't know. I pray to God I didn't.

Statements that he can't remember include the following:

— Wishes that he could
— Expressions that he is being honest with police
— Requests for police to be honest with him
— Self-blame
— Religious language (*God, pray*)

Eight times, Alben tells the interrogation team that he can't remember what happened that night. On the fifth of these, he pleads with the officers to tell *him* what happened. Alben is convinced that they know but refuse to tell him. He says that he wishes he could recall the events of that night, that he is being honest about this, and that he blames himself for not knowing.

To this point, Bruce and I have been building our case for Alben's consistency. He is consistent throughout in not admitting the attack, and he consistently says he cannot remember anything about it. The next question concerns Alben's consistency about remembering things before he blacked out and on the following day. To display what Alben says he remembered, I constructed a chart titled "Temporal Discourse Sequencing." It divided all the statements Alben made in the interrogation into five time periods: the recent past, at the restaurant, at the racetrack, after leaving the racetrack, and the next day, as follows:

Alben Recalls

Recent Past	At Restaurant	At Track	After Leaving Track	Next Day
wife burned self	he had corned beef	where they parked		waking up
				shirts knocked down
had tools in car	he had martinis	went inside		
		didn't stay till end		turned off TV
clothes in car	he finished wife's drink	not feeling well		walked into front room
blacked out before				
	he argued with wife	had a few more drinks		went to bathroom
	took Buick	wife was winning		opened screen on window for air
		pled with her to go		she wasn't there
				her car was gone
				called mother-in-law
				mother-in-law came
				looked down street
				called lots of people: Valerie, Julie, Cari
				went to hospital for chest pain

Once again, throughout the interrogation, Alben is consistent in that he never recalls anything in the crucial time slot, after leaving the track. But he also makes statements about what he does not remember. Using the same five time frames, the following items were charted:

Alben Does Not Recall

Recent Past	At Restaurant	At Track	After Leaving Track	Next Day
where in car he left hammer	what wife ate how much bill was		getting into car	
whether wife had velvety jacket			going into house	
			turning off TV	
			where he sat in car	
			whether they dropped Valerie at home	
			anything after they left	
			hitting his wife	

There is a perfect match in the column After Leaving Track. He remembers nothing and does not remember seven things asked of him by the police. There is nothing that he fails to remember on the day after the attack (the same day as his interrogation). In contrast, he fails to remember two things asked of him that transpired at the restaurant and two things in the recent past. These responses were not crucial to the case, however, and proved of no consequence. It is understandable not to recall what one's wife ordered at a restaurant and quite possible to forget the total of the bill. He freely admitted having tools in his car, mostly to use on his boat. He admits having a hammer in the car, but he does not recall whether it was in the trunk or on the floor of the back seat. It is understandable that a man might not recall items in his wife's wardrobe, especially if she was not wearing it the day before.

This examination of Alben's consistency then was completed. He makes no contradictory statement even while describing what he recalls over five time frames. I could not prove that he was truthful, but I could find no language evidence that would spot holes in his story or cast doubt on his honesty. There may be no way to see into Alben's mind and know that he is telling the truth, but we hoped that by meticulously inspecting his statement for any clues to lying and finding none, we could accomplish the same results. Because we had no indication that Alben was an accomplished (or even an amateur) con artist, we hoped to convert his candid revelations of his recent arguments with his wife from a deficit to a strength. Only an accomplished con artist would be so brazen and skillful as to volunteer a potential motive to the prosecution as a means to convincing the government that by doing so he or she was innocent. The average Joe or Jane would never think of this. An accomplished con artist would admit something that is unimportant as a way of establishing credibility, but even a professional con man would not be likely to go so far as to admit that his relationship with his wife was strained. Alben admitted all this, obviously, because it was the truth.

Even this admission of problems with his wife is consistent with other unnecessary admissions Alben made in his statement. There was no particular reason for him to admit having unreported income, for example. But when asked about his salary, he volunteered that he made money from coin-operated laundry machines that did not appear on his income tax forms. It is difficult to imagine any motive for Alben's saying this other than a conscientious effort to be forthright. And if he was forthright about his unreported income, why wouldn't he be forthright about everything else? The defense position, of course, was that he was. I could not testify that Alben was telling the truth in his interrogation, but I could testify that he was completely consistent in what he said, contrary to most people who lie. It is possible, I suppose, that Alben was actually a very accomplished liar who had his story down pat and consistently stuck to it. But nothing in Alben's background supports this theory. In any case, his interrogation came too close on the heels of the discovery of his wife's death to allow for artful planning of a story. And if a murderer were to construct an alibi, he would not be likely to choose the one Alben described. He might have constructed a story about hearing mysterious noises in the night, about seeing someone flee in the darkness. Or he could have arranged to be seen by some people to establish an alibi. One of the weakest stories imaginable is the one Alben told, simply because he cannot deny that he did it; he can only say that he has no memory of anything. Our theory was that an accomplished liar would have done better than this.

Alben's truthfulness in his "confession" statement was to be a central part of his defense. The event that led up to the prosecutor's reconsidering his indictment took place 13 years prior to legal action. During this period, the police remained undecided about whether they had a case against him. As the time of trial came closer, those same doubts must have recycled because charges were dropped and the case never came to trial.

▶ Was Jessie Moffett Lying?

The question of Jessie Moffett's constitutional rights was discussed in Chapter 3. The major issue in this case, however, was whether Moffett was telling the truth in his police interrogations.

To review briefly, on April 12, 1979, the mutilated body of a white female named Deborah Owens was discovered near the Linda Vista Recreation Center in Southern California. A San Diego Police Department homicide unit investigated the case as soon as the body was discovered and had no immediate suspects. The following day, however, a neighbor, Jessie Moffett, called detective Richard A. Carey, then a member of the investigating unit. As a result of this telephone call, Moffett became a suspect in that homicide. Detective Carey arranged to meet Moffett at the recreation center, a meeting that Carey said took less than 2 hours. On April 17, the San Diego Police contacted numerous people concerning this murder, one of them being Moffett once again. After questioning him at his home for a while, at about 6 p.m. Carey decided to take Moffett to police headquarters, where police advised him of his rights and let him go at 4:00 on the morning of April 18. Moffett was never charged in court with the homicide in 1979. Some 3 months later, Moffett became a prime suspect in a rape case, and Detective Carey once again went to the district attorney to get a complaint for the murder of Deborah Owens. Both complaints were originally canceled by the San Diego Police for lack of evidence against Moffett although he was later convicted in the rape case.

In April 1979, the San Diego Police also interrogated another resident of that area, Derrick Pritchett, on several occasions. The first time was on the same night as Moffett's original interview, April 18, 1979. Moffett had been brought to the police station at 6 p.m. and interrogated for approximately 1 hour and 10 minutes. The detective at this interrogation states on tape that the concluding time was 9:08 p.m. on April 17 although the cover sheet lists the time as between 6 p.m. and 1 a.m. of April 18.

Between 1:27 a.m. and 2:25 a.m. on April 18, Pritchett was interrogated while Moffett was left waiting in another room. At 3:30 a.m., Moffett and Pritchett were placed in the back seat of a police car alone. Unbeknownst to them, the police had activated a tape recorder in an effort to capture inculpatory conversation between the two suspects. This tape recording was ruled inadmissible as evidence in the case against Moffett, and it is doubtful, at any rate, what good it would have been to the government.

Because the surreptitious tape placed by Detective Carey in the back seat of the car may have yielded no results that were positive concerning Moffett's guilt, and because the court ruled that the tape was inadmissible anyway, the police proceeded in another direction: to Derrick Pritchett.

Over the years, the San Diego Police continued to interrogate Pritchett about his involvement in the murder of Deborah Owens. Pritchett had originally admitted that he was with Jessie Moffett on the night of the murder, but he also claimed that he had nothing to do with it. Similar to the case of DeWayne Hill (see Chapter 6), Pritchett's confession of his own and Moffett's involvement changed dramatically over time (and occasionally even within a given interrogation). From 1979 to 1990, Pritchett was interrogated on four occasions.

Linguists, like other scientists, are trained to describe, compare, categorize, and analyze their data. When the data consist of words and sentences, such analysis becomes, by definition, linguistic analysis. Interrogations, like conversations, consist of continuous discourse between two or more speakers. In normal conversation, each speaker has the right and ability to bring up new topics or to cut off old ones. In an interrogation, the rules are somewhat different. Investigators have the power in an interrogation, and they control the topics being introduced. They ask the questions. They decide when to start and stop. They have the right to interrupt. The suspect has none of this power.

Scientists search for patterns when they analyze data, noting recurring similarities and differences. When language is the data, the most obvious recurring patterns are found in responses to the same topics throughout the different samples of data. In the case of the four interrogations of Pritchett, significant variation was found in Pritchett's responses in nine topics.

	Dates			
Topics	4-18-79	8-2-79	4-30-80	8-1-90
• where DP met JM	• left Odom's house together	• at the Jack-in-the-Box	• at the Jack-in-the-Box	• at Rec Center or Jack-in-the-Box
• persons present and seen on stroll	• J. Moffett D. Pritchett	• Unidentified male J. Moffett D. Pritchett	• J. Moffett D. Pritchett dead girl	• J. Moffett D. Pritchett dead girl Julie Wendy
• hear a scream?	• not mentioned	• JM: heard it DP: no	• JM: heard it DP: no	• JM: heard it DP: no

	Dates			
Topics	4-18-79	8-2-79	4-30-80	8-1-90
JM's T-shirt	• JM "probably said" he had to take T-shirt off to help girl • doesn't recall if JM had shirt on	• thinks JM had shirt off	• JM shirt had blood and dirt on it • JM not wearing T-shirt • Not sure • JM wore T-shirt • No, T-shirt was in hand • JM wearing T-shirt • No, he was not	• JM holding T-shirt
see blood	• No blood on T-shirt • No bloodstain on JM's shirt	• Doesn't recall commenting on blood on JM's T-shirt • No blood on JM's shirt • Doesn't recall asking JM where blood on shirt came from "but that's probably what I said."	• I said, "How'd you get blood on you?" • told me he wiped girl's face off • It had blood and dirt on it.	• told me he wiped blood from girl's face
see girl	• didn't see girl	• I think JM was going to check on *that* broad • He told me there's a girl back there, beaten. • He's going to check up • said broad lying there screaming	• I seen her lying in ditch looking wild, in ditch, • He said it looked like she'd been raped • I don't recall him saying there is this girl back there had just been raped or she's dead. • I thought she was dead.	• Jessie said he saw girl in ditch with a brick on her head. • I saw the girl in ditch • Next morning, I walked by ditch and saw girl still there.

	Dates			
Topics	4-18-79	8-2-79	4-30-80	8-1-90
• Jessie's direction	• not sure which way he went • not sure where he went	• JM went toward back of park, walked around tennis courts	• walked by basketball court, past tennis court and back by racquetball court • heads toward racquetball court—see his foots • going that way, came back this way	• JM walked away from us toward buildings in park • I didn't see where he went
• DP waited what DP did in park	• 15-20 minutes waited for Moffett in park	• 5 minutes stayed right there on bench	• 5 minutes I said I would stay and wait for him	• 10-15 minutes I walked to ditch with JM

In the light of these nine factual differences in Pritchett's sworn testimony over an 11-year period, what can be said about truthfulness? Earlier, I said that linguistic analysis cannot diagnose lying. But careful comparison can most certainly point out inconsistency.

Details Added

In five of the nine fact descriptions compared above, Pritchett's responses indicate that his memory apparently improves over time, contrary to everything that is known in memory research.

PERSONS PRESENT

In April, what started out as two persons present or seen (on their stroll through the park) increases to three by August, changes to a different three people by the following April, and becomes five people in 1990.

HEAR SCREAM

No scream was mentioned in the initial interview, and then Pritchett consistently says Moffett heard a scream, whereas he, Pritchett, did not.

SEE BLOOD

No blood was seen in April 1979. But by August, Pritchett not only does not recall asking Moffett about blood on his T-shirt but also does not recall even mentioning the subject the previous April. One year later, however, Pritchett's memory has improved to the point that he now not only recalls asking Moffett about the blood but also even remembers his own exact words as well as Moffett's response (that he used his T-shirt to wipe blood from the girl's face). This gain in memory precision diminishes somewhat by 1990 but retains the gist of his April 1980 recall.

DIDN'T SEE THE GIRL

In the initial interrogation, Pritchett says he did not see the girl at all. By August, he refers to *that* broad who Moffett said was lying back there, beaten and screaming. By April 1980, Pritchett now recalls actually seeing the girl lying in a ditch, looking wild. Pritchett thought she was dead but contradicts himself about whether Moffett said she had been raped. Ten years later, Pritchett recalls Moffett saying the girl had a brick on her head and still maintains that he also saw the girl, adding that he also went back the next morning to see her in the ditch.

WHAT PRITCHETT DID IN THE PARK

In April 1979, Pritchett says only that he waited in the park while Moffett went off to investigate the scream. By August 1979, Pritchett recalls that he waited on the bench. By April 1980, he adds that he told Moffett he would stay and wait for him. But by August 1990, Pritchett now recalls that he walked with Moffett to the ditch to see the girl.

Details Change but Eventually Same as Original

In two of Pritchett's nine fact descriptions compared here, Pritchett's memory changes and then returns to his original statement, as follows:

THE DIRECTION JESSIE WENT

In April 1979, Pritchett isn't sure in which direction Moffett walked in the park. Four months later, he recalls that Moffett went toward the back of the park, around the tennis courts. In April 1980, he adds that Moffett walked by the basketball court, past the tennis court, and back by the racquetball court. Now, he recalls seeing Moffett's feet. By August 1990, an atrophy of memory occurs, and Pritchett is back to not knowing for sure exactly where Jessie went.

HOW LONG PRITCHETT WAITED

In April 1979, Pritchett said he waited for 15 to 20 minutes while Moffett went to investigate the scream. In August 1979 and April 1980, this had reduced to 5 minutes, but in August 1990, Pritchett recalls the time as 10 to 15 minutes, closer to the original statement.

Details Inconsistent Throughout

Pritchett is most inconsistent in his four statements regarding Moffett's T-shirt. On this topic, Pritchett is as inconsistent within his statements as he is across them. On April 18, 1979, Pritchett doesn't recall whether Moffett had a T-shirt on, but oddly enough, he also states that Moffett "probably said" that he had to take his T-shirt off to help the girl. In April 1980, however, Pritchett is at his inconsistent best. First, he says Moffett's shirt had blood on it, and then he says Moffett was not wearing a T-shirt. Next, he says he's not sure whether Moffett was wearing a T-shirt. Then, he says Moffett was wearing a T-shirt. Then, he corrects this and says that Moffett was holding his T-shirt in his hand. Next, he says Moffett was wearing the T-shirt. Finally, he says that Moffett did not wear a T-shirt. Ten years later, Pritchett says Moffett held his T-shirt in his hands.

From Pritchett's four interrogations by the San Diego Police, then, we can see three patterns of inconsistency. In the majority of these fact statements, Pritchett's memory seems to improve over time, quite in contrast to everything that is known about gradual memory deterioration. On other topics, Pritchett's memory changes over time, only to return in the end to his original recall of the topic. Finally, Pritchett is inconsistent, even within the same interrogation, about the facts that he reports.

Derrick Pritchett's testimony was crucial to the prosecution of Jessie Moffett in the murder of Deborah Owens. Contrastive analysis of Pritchett's responses indicated inconsistency across time and even within statements themselves. Linguistic analysis, in this matter, consisted of a contrastive analysis of the statements uttered by Pritchett in his four interrogations over a time span of 11 years. From all that is known about memory, Pritchett's memory should have decreased over time. In the majority of topics here, this was not true. Is it possible that Pritchett's memory actually improved over time? Nothing in the research on memory would suggest this, leaving us with a quandary. Is Derrick Pritchett the lone exception to human ability to lose factual memory over time? Or is Derrick Pritchett a liar?

Moffett's defense attorney, Geraldine Russell, believed that Pritchett was lying. Linguistic analysis of the inconsistency of his statements supported her belief. Linguistic analysis has no internal mind-probing capability—only the careful and time-consuming hard work of comparative analysis. Eventually, Moffett was tried and convicted of first-degree murder. The tapes of Pritchett's interrogations were eventually ruled inadmissible, along with the surreptitious tape of the conversation between Moffett and Pritchett in the back seat of a police car. Curiously enough, these two tapes offered perhaps the most exculpatory evidence.

In both the Alben and the Moffett cases, linguistic analysis addressed the issue of possible deceptive language by determining the consistencies and inconsistencies found in the actual language being used by both interrogator and subject, rather than through the more reductionist, experimental methods used by previous research studies. Experimental studies attempt to isolate individual features of verbal and nonverbal language, usually by gathering subjects' reactions to such features under experimental conditions. As noted earlier, Miller and Stiff (1993), in assessing the progress of such studies, claim that a coin flip would provide almost equally valid results. Considerably less esoteric, but on far more solid ground, is the comparison of subjects' statements at one time with those statements at later times. On equally solid ground is the linguist's analysis of the influence of questions on answers. All questions are coercive in some sense. It is the method and degree to which they are coercive that linguistic analysis can prove helpful to the trier of the facts.

Language of
Written Confessions

I n the cases involving tape-recorded confessions described earlier, I
focused on the perceptions and misperceptions of the police and
their techniques of questioning Steve Allen and Chris Jerue, the
apparent restructuring of Judge Goltz's statement, language issues in the DWI
(driving while intoxicated) arrests, and questions about the waiver of rights
by Jessie Moffett and Charles Lorraine. But when the major confession
evidence against a suspect is a written confession, this opens up a somewhat
different type of linguistic analysis: stylistics. Describing forensic stylistics,
McMenamin (1993) says, "Author-specific linguistic patterns are present in
unique combinations in the styles of every writer, and these underlying
patterns can be objectively described and often measured by careful observation and analysis, making author identification possible in many cases"
(p. xiii).

Stylistics is the analysis of patterns of variation in language, long recognized as a tool in determining the authorship of literary works. In the legal
setting, stylistics is often used in alleged forgery cases and to determine the
authorship of documents. Categories such as spelling, morphology, syntax,
punctuation, word choice, and abbreviations provide the features that linguists
examine and compare (see McMenamin, 1993, for a detailed list of such
features).

It is most common to compare documents of known authorship with
documents whose authorship is disputed. No single feature of style is adequate
to make such a judgment, but a clustering of similar or different features or
both can lead to the conclusion that it is likely that a given person wrote or
did not write the document in question. Stylistic analysis is not foolproof, and

the best a linguist can do is give an educated estimate of the likelihood of his or her opinion being accurate. But then, that is what expert opinion means.

► Michael Carter's Written Statement

In some states, it has become standard procedure to tape-record murder confessions. This practice does not preclude also obtaining signed written confessions, however, because as Inbau et al. (1986) point out, written confessions seem to be more convincing to juries than are tape-recorded presentations (p. 176). In some cases, both spoken and written confessions have been obtained from the same suspect. Such was the situation in a first-degree murder trial in Louisiana in 1989.

Michael T. Carter is a young black man who spent 434 days in jail on first-degree murder charges and was then released after the prosecution finally admitted that his indictment "was based in significant part on evidence which was later determined to be inaccurate." The prosecutors eventually realized, at least in part because of a linguistic analysis of his alleged confession, the error of Carter's indictment and incarceration.

In February 1989, I was called by Carter's attorney, Michele Fournet, from Baton Rouge. She explained the basic background of the case, including the fact that a white motorcycle officer had been shot and killed by a young black male in a predominantly white section of the city. Many suspects were brought in for interrogation until, finally, the police decided that Michael Carter was the prime candidate.

The interrogation of Michael Carter was tape-recorded, and that tape, along with a transcript prepared by the police, was presented as evidence that Carter had indeed committed the murder. Attorney Fournet's request to me was simply, "Is there anything a linguist can contribute to Carter's defense?" My response was that I didn't know but that I would be happy to examine the interrogation tape and the written confession and see what I could find.

My previous experience in analyzing police interrogations led me to look carefully for linguistic evidence of undue persuasion, even coercion, by the police. Amazing as it may seem, I have also learned that what the police call a confession often differs markedly from what others may consider this speech act to be. Sometimes the accused confess to something far different from the murder with which they are accused, and the case goes to trial anyway, just as though they had confessed to the homicide.

The first step of the linguist in all cases involving tape-recorded evidence is to listen to the tapes carefully and correct the transcripts of those tapes. I have yet to discover a perfect transcript, even by the relatively simple standards of the courts. Whether produced by the prosecution or by the defense, such transcripts are not usually made by language professionals who are trained to hear simultaneous speech, overlapping, or a range of dialectal speech or who understand the significance of pause length, pause fillers, feedback markers such as *uh-huh* and *OK,* and many other significant conversational markers. Nor do the traditional transcribers often have access to the equipment necessary for producing an accurate transcript, such as AKG earphones or tape decks such as the Nakamichi CR7A, the Bang and Olufsen Beocord 9000, or the Marantz PMD 200, which has the capability of varying the pitch and speed of speech so that one can more readily determine negative contractions from positive ones, such as *can* from *can't.*

The government's transcript of this interrogation was flawed in many ways, not the least of which was the inaccurate identification of speakers. Once a transcript is made jury-ready and as accurate as possible, the next step is to call on any analytical tool available to describe with integrity and accuracy just exactly what was going on in the conversation.

As in the Alben case, described in Chapter 4, one crucial analysis is that of the speech acts of denying and accusing. In the 40 minutes in which Carter was interrogated on tape, he denied 10 times that he shot the officer. In a hearing to suppress the confession as evidence in this case, I presented the following simple chart of Carter's denials:

Carter Denies Shooting Anyone

p. 1	Didn't do it.
p. 2	I didn't do it.
p. 3	I didn't shoot nobody, though.
p. 3	I didn't shoot nobody.
p. 3	I didn't shoot at nobody, though.
p. 7	I didn't shoot him, though.
p. 7	I didn't shoot him.
p. 9	I didn't shoot him.
p. 9	I didn't shoot him.
p. 12	I didn't know I shot him the first time (in response to the question, "Why did you shoot him a second time?").

At no time during the tape-recorded interrogation did Carter ever admit to shooting anyone. What he did admit to was accompanying two other young men on bicycles to the place near where the officer was shot. He admitted that their intent was to rob houses and that his role was to be the lookout while the other two did the jobs.

Another speech act I analyzed was that of accusing. The interrogating officers, five in all, accused Carter of lying, maintaining that he did indeed shoot the officer. The instances of this were as follows:

Officers Accuse Carter

p. 2	MC:	I didn't shoot nobody, though.
	OP:	Yes you did, Michael.
p. 3	MC:	I didn't shoot nobody.
	OP:	Michael, tell us the truth.
p. 7	OP:	Michael, the gun did not go off when you threw it.
p. 9	OP:	You fired the gun, Michael . . . and it did not go off when you threw it.
p. 9	OP:	It did not go off when you threw it. It can't happen.
p. 10	OP:	He was shot by a left-handed man. You're left-handed.
p. 10	OW:	What made you shoot him, Michael?
p. 11	MC:	I ain't know what happened.
	OP:	No, no, Michael. You know what happened. You know exactly what happened.
p. 12	OW:	OK. He was on the ground. The gun was in your hand, and what did you do then?
	MC:	Ran.
	OM:	No, Michael.
	OP:	No, no, Michael. You shot twice.
p. 12	OW:	Michael, why did you feel it necessary to shoot him the second time?
p. 13	OW:	So before you ran, you fired again.
p. 15	OW:	You get enough blood on them? (clothing)
p. 19	MC:	Didn't see him go down.
	OP:	You seen him go down.

The prosecutor argued that it is the nature of such interrogations for police officers to accuse the suspect. However true this may be, both the psychiatrist-expert witness and I independently responded that such procedure was not conducive to getting at the truth and that the officers' interviewing strategies would be considered counterproductive, no matter what topic or field. We both described the need to begin with open-ended questions before moving sequentially to *wh-* questions and finally, only if necessary for probing purposes, to yes-no questions. Both expert witnesses independently argued in favor of questions that permit a suspect to self-generate answers, rather than be influenced by the question type, as exemplified by the many tag questions used by the police in this interrogation.

To this point in my testimony, I had explained that the police interviewing procedure was highly flawed and coercive, containing mostly accusations, whereas Carter's major topic was to deny any guilt in the shooting. Of particular interest was that even though the police referred to this event as a "confession to murder," no such confession was there. But there *was* the matter of the signed confession statement, a handwritten document in which the police, under oath, claimed they merely wrote down Carter's exact words as he spoke them. The question here was whether Carter actually said what the police say he said. Did they construct this confession themselves and then ask or even induce Carter to sign it?

The test of the truth of the police officers' claim was found in the language used. We have a sample of Carter's language in the tape recording. We also have a sample of the police officers' language there. But, in addition, we also have samples of the police officers' language in various hearings that had preceded this one. Although it was not always possible to identify the voices of all five police officers in the interrogation, two of them had distinctive voices that even the government's transcript identified accurately: Officer A and Officer B. Because Officer A dominated among the five interrogating police officers, it became apparent that it might be fruitful to compare his language use with that of the written confession to determine whether the words ascribed to Carter were his own, as Officer A had testified, or whether they were actually the words of Officer A.

At this point, then, I carried out a contrastive analysis of the language found in the taped interrogation with the language of the written confession. Following is the comparison of such language used in my testimony at the suppression hearing:

Comparison of Interrogation With Written Statement

		Interrogation	Written Confession
1. (p. 1)	OA: MC:	You and Lobo and Kermit left, right, Michael? Yeah.	Myself, my cousin Lobo, Freddie Mills, and Kermit Parker left me and Lobo's house.
2. (p. 1)	MC:	Kermit came over to this, to this here (inaudible) . . . I don't know where it is over there.	. . . and went over to the neighborhood off Woodale.
3. (p. 1)	MC:	It was on the way there. They say we can have them here and take them quickly to run over there. All I was supposed to do is, is keep an eye on the bicycles . . . then talk, them talking about going to this, we should hit this neighborhood. I was supposed to be look- out man.	Kermit and Lobo were going to try to break into some houses, and I was supposed to watch out for them
4. (p. 5)	MC:	He told all of us to lay down on our stomachs and have our hands up.	He made us lay face down and put our hands up.
5. (p.10)	OA: MC:	It had the thing—the round thing where you put the bullets in. Yes.	. . . and a round thing you put the bullets in.
6. (p. 10)	OB: OA:	What happened to make you shoot him? Did you think you were fixing to get shot?	I thought he was going to shoot me.
7. (p. 10)	MC:	I froze for a while.	We both froze for a moment.
8. (p. 10)	MC: OA: MC:	He had turned around quick. You had the gun in your hand, didn't you? Yes.	But the cop turned around, and I had the gun still in my hand.
9. (p. 12)	MC: OA: MC:	I don't know what happened. He was on the ground. Was the gun in your hand when he went down? (crying, no response)	The gun I had went off, and the next thing I knew the motorcycle cop was down.

Interrogation	Written Confession
10. MC: Kermit had the gun. Kermit (p. 12) had it under his pants under his shirt.	Kermit had a pistol in his pants.

The comparison shows several types of differences between what Carter said in the taped interrogation and what he is alleged to have said for the written statement. In Examples 1, 5, 6, and 8, for example, the officer's utterance in the interview is ascribed to Carter in the written confession. Even though Carter appears to be agreeing to these statements by the officer, the words are those of the police and not those of Carter, and we should keep in mind that Officer A testified under oath that he wrote down only Carter's own words and sentences.

The second comparative difference between the interrogation and the written statement consists of details left out in the tape but supplied in the writing. Examples 2 and 7 illustrate this. Carter doesn't know the name of the street in the interrogation but identifies it as Woodale in the written statement. The prosecution remained unclear whether all of Carter's written statements were uttered after they had turned off the tape recorder, whether they had patched together Carter's sentences from the taped interview, or whether some combination of these approaches obtained. It could be possible that Carter finally recalled the street name in an untaped part of the interrogation, but no such claim was made, nor was any reason given why the tape recorder was not turned back on when, and if, the alleged confession statement was dictated.

The third type of language contrast here consists of the upgrading of Carter's language to a more middle-class, police language orientation. Examples of this are found in 1 ("Myself"), 3 ("break into"), 4 ("lay face down"), and 7 ("for a moment"). Nowhere in Carter's tape-recorded speech can such terms be found. To check for this further, I had the attorney tape-record another hour of conversation with Carter in his jail cell. These expressions were never used. They appear, instead, to be police language.

In fact, in his deposition, Officer A consistently used the reflexive pronoun *myself* as part of a compound subject (e.g., "Officer B and myself went out"). This is a common hypercorrection of the middle-class speaker who has vague knowledge of the fact that *me* is an improper sentence subject but who has not yet mastered when or how to use *I*. There is nothing middle class about Carter's speech that would suggest such language awareness. Likewise, Carter never used the phrasal possessive, suggested in the written statement by "left me and Lobo's house," suggesting strongly that these were not Carter's dictated words.

The last type of language contrast is found in Example 8. Carter had admitted that Kermit threw him a gun after they were apprehended and that Carter immediately threw the gun into some bushes. If the gun went off at all, about which Carter was uncertain, he reasoned that it must have discharged when it hit the ground. Example 8 shows much ambiguity about the time reference surrounding this event. In the interrogation, Carter agreed that he had the gun in his hand briefly because he caught it when Kermit threw it to him. The police did not attempt to clarify this timing during the interrogation but conveniently interpreted it only one way in the written statement, even adding the word *still*. Nor was it ever established that this event with a gun was in any way connected with the event in which the officer was shot.

In the next portion of my testimony, I compared the syntax of Carter with that of Officer A, who had admitted in his deposition that he was the amanuensis for Carter's signed, written confession. In courtroom testimony about linguistic analysis, I have found that it is best to keep the analysis as simple as possible. I could have done elaborate clause depth analyses, but I feared that such an approach would not be understood. Instead, I opted for analytical categories that were more familiar: the simple, compound, and complex sentence usage of Carter and Officer A. To do this, I simply tabulated all the sentences in the written statement with those in Carter's interrogation and compared their frequency, as follows:

Comparison of Carter's Syntax in Interrogation With Syntax of Written Statement

Sentence Type	Carter in Interrogation	Written Statement
Simple	81%	32%
Compound	8%	48%
Complex	11%	20%

The contrast is dramatic. Somehow, if Carter actually dictated the statement, he reduced his preponderance of simple sentences by two thirds and increased his compound sentences sixfold. This possibility in itself is unlikely and casts serious doubt on the accuracy of Officer A's claim to be a mere amanuensis. In my testimony, I called special attention to the following sentence allegedly dictated by Carter and transcribed by Officer A:

As we were on the street looking at houses to break in, a cop came up on a motorcycle and started checking us.

This complex sentence containing an initial dependent clause is nothing like the language actually used by Michael Carter in the tape recordings.

Having shown that the language known to be Michael Carter's on the tape-recorded interrogation is unlike that represented to be his own in the allegedly dictated written confession, I then compared the syntax of Officer A in his turns of talk in the interrogation and in his testimony with that of this written statement, as follows:

Officer A's Syntax

Sentence Type	Officer A's Interrogation	Officer A's Testimony
Simple	38%	43%
Compound	27%	26%
Complex	35%	31%

Noteworthy here is Officer A's consistency of syntactic usage across events, tasks, and time. So similar are his frequencies, in fact, that they suggest a kind of grammatical signature. Having presented this in court, Attorney Fournet then asked me:

Q: Does the sentence structure that appears in the written statement resemble the sentence structure used by Michael Carter when Michael Carter speaks?

A: Not at all.

Q: Whose sentence structure does it resemble in this scenario involving these people?

A: Well, I don't mean to pick on Officer A, but since he said he wrote it down, it's closer to his sentence structure than it is to that of Mr. Carter.

Q: How much closer?

A: A lot closer.

Finally, Attorney Fournet asked me to elaborate on the term *signature*, which I had used in reference to the grammatical consistency of Officer A's syntax across events, topics, and times. I explained that such signatures can be found in any aspect of language use: pronunciation, vocabulary choice, or grammar. The linguist describes individual word signatures, for example, as well as the more unconscious grammatical patterns. Earlier, I had noted that the reflexive pronoun *myself* did not comport with Carter's usage, yet it appears in the written statement allegedly dictated by Carter. This finding led me to search for the reflexive pronoun in Officer A's testimony, where I found the following:

Officer A's Hearing Testimony

p. 43	The police officers involved including myself, Det. B, Det. C . . .
p. 43	I drove by with him in the car, myself, Det. D . . .
p. 48	At various times myself, Det. D, Det. B . . .
p. 67	By several people including myself . . .
p. 69	Myself and Det. B . . .
p. 70	Myself, Det. B . . .
p. 70	Myself, Det. E, Det. D . . .

I concluded this portion of my testimony by pointing out that when comparative analysis of this type is used, no single feature is adequate to offer certainty about authorship attribution but that a combination of such features leads to the inescapable conclusion I reached here. The final question, to me, was as follows:

Q: Just generally based on everything you've said, Dr. Shuy, and based on your examination of all these items and documents, how likely is it that the words that appear on that written statement are the words of Michael Carter?

A: It's very unlikely that these were Michael Carter's words.

Q: How likely is it that the words that appear on that written statement are instead the words of Officer A?

A: It is much more likely that these were his words, especially in light of the fact that he said that he was the person who wrote them down.

Five months after this testimony, the chief trial attorney for the district attorney's office filed a motion to dismiss the grand jury indictment of Michael Carter. This motion concluded, "Recent developments reveal that further investigation is required in order to prosecute effectively the offense which was committed." This motion to dismiss was submitted on the day that the judge was to give his ruling on the motion to suppress the confession of which my testimony was a part.

The written confession is highly regarded by law enforcement agencies for a number of reasons. One, it focuses on the salient issues, guilt in particular, and contains little of the distracting conversational interaction found in tape-recorded conversations. Two, the written confession avoids the appearance of leading questions on the part of the interrogator because the entire question-answer format of the interrogation can be converted, in a written confession, to a first-person narrative. Three, narrative evidence is more convincing to juries, particularly if it is coherent and does not ramble. Four, the written confession also eliminates the many yes-no questions that often dominate interrogations.

Inbau et al.'s (1986) advice to police interrogators on the elicitation of written confessions is for the police to use the confessor's own language:

> In the preparation of the written confession no attempt should be made to improve the language used by the subject himself. It should represent his confession as he tells it, and unless it does, a judge or jury may be reluctant to believe that a defendant whose education may have ended at the third grade spoke the language of a college graduate. (p. 131)

The fact that Officer A testified under oath that he wrote down Carter's words exactly as he had spoken them was the key to Carter's defense even though the confession was signed by Carter. The tape-recorded statement was very helpful because it gave clear clues to why Carter signed it. He broke into sobs on more than one occasion and even became very ill during his interrogation. He was obviously in no physical or emotional condition to comprehend what he had signed, and the linguistic analysis made it clear that the text itself was not Carter's creation.

▶ The Written Statement as a Clue to Deception

Written statements are approached from a quite different perspective by Avinoam Sapir (1987), who created the *scientific content analysis (SCAN)* technique, used not only by personnel at his laboratory but also by many law enforcement agencies whose personnel he has trained. Sapir's approach is to have subjects write statements (about what they know happened) before they are even interviewed. From such written statements, usually about 1½ pages long, he carefully inspects the language used in the statements and narrows down the suspect list to a manageable few subjects to be interviewed, thereby saving much time and effort on the part of law enforcement agencies. The underlying analytical principles of the SCAN analysis are similar to some aspects of what is treated in this book, the major difference being that the analyses shown in this book were carried out on existing oral interrogations. Sapir agrees that interrogations are often highly flawed. Whereas I argue that such flaws can be repaired by various methods, Sapir would turn the process on its head, with the written statement first and the interview following, only if justified. Despite this quite different beginning point, however, much can be said for the essential principles of both approaches.

Sapir's SCAN approach assumes that the interviewer is the most serious obstacle to obtaining information. On this, there can be little disagreement, as illustrated by the case studies in this book. There is also no disagreement about the fact that the best evidence is that where the subjects are freely permitted to generate their own guilt, usually with open-ended questions (also advocated by most police manuals but, from my experience, seldom followed in practice). In essence, the initial written statement for which Sapir argues provides exactly the kind of self-generated opportunity the good interrogation should produce, especially at the onset of the interview. There is complete agreement, as well, that any statement, written or spoken, has two types of information: content information and language information. Most linguistic work in confession cases has focused on content inconsistencies more than on any specific language that might indicate deception, and for good reason. Linguistic analysis cannot say for sure that a person is deceptive. It can point to potentially deceptive language, which is what Sapir's SCAN does, but the ultimate validation of deceptive language can be achieved only after content facts are known to be inconsistent or false. In all fairness to SCAN, no claim is made that subjects whose statements are judged to have produced potentially deceptive language are actually lying. As noted earlier, SCAN uses such language as a guide to the interviewer about what to probe, what to challenge, and what to disbelieve in the follow-up interrogation.

Rabon (1994) developed an interviewing technique called *investigative discourse analysis (IDA),* which in many ways parallels Sapir's approach. Rabon also starts with the subject's narrative but, unlike Sapir, will work with the subject's spoken narrative or even with one dictated by the subject and written down by the investigator. Both Sapir and Rabon aver that a subject's lack of conviction about what he or she says is revealed by his or her modifying or equivocating terms. Such subjects are reluctant to refer to past events in the past tense, they relate events vaguely, they avoid self-referencing, and they produce a quantitative imbalance between the three salient parts of a narration (prologue, main event, epilogue). Fewer words per sentence in the narration of the main event than in the other parts of the narrative is another indicator of deception, according to these training programs.

The linguist can agree that many language features singled out by both Sapir and Rabon could be significant, especially if the contexts in which language is used could be controlled for culture, occupation, age, ethnicity, gender, education, geography, and other confounding variables. For example, both Rabon and Sapir make much of a subject's switch from past tense to present tense narration, whereas American speech practice reveals that many people use the historical present tense in narratives that have nothing to do with crimes. Likewise, both Sapir and Rabon find evidence of deceit in a switch in reference from, for example, "Jim" to "my partner," or "Janie" to "my wife," despite the stylistic rule learned by many speakers of English that one should avoid using the same terms in proximity.

Sapir's SCAN and Rabon's IDA techniques (others have names like the *kinesic interview technique* and *statement analysis*) have many other useful and important aspects, but it is not appropriate here to go into detail. Suffice it to say that some law enforcement agencies claim to have benefited from them. It should remain very clear, however, that these approaches do not successfully identify specific deceitful language. They may somehow help narrow down lists of suspects, but the individual language features they describe deal with the variety of cultures, genders, socioeconomic groups, education levels, or occupations/professions of subjects as though they were all one.

Language of the
Implicational Confession

6

People confess for a number of reasons. Some confess because it expunges their guilt over doing a bad thing. Others confess because it makes them feel important to have done such a monstrous thing. Still others confess to small things to throw off their interrogators about the really big things. Perhaps most troublesome of all, however, are the persons who confess to a crime to implicate others in the same violation. Their reasons for doing this vary: They may simply want to get even with the persons they implicate even though confessions of their own part in the crime could send them to prison. Usually in such cases, what the confessors admit to is much less serious than that of the person they implicate. This is why police investigators try hard to get the driver of the getaway car to admit guilt first so that he or she will then tell them who the actual bank robbers were. If law enforcement officers can get the little guy to flip, their work is half over and their task is much easier to accomplish. Armed with the driver's confession and implication of the other participants, the interrogators have the essential tools to finish their case.

▶ Surrogate Confession of DeWayne Hill

One such implicational confession took place in Monroe, Louisiana, beginning in September 1989. An elderly woman, Ms. Elnora Coon, had been brutally murdered and her body found on the floor of her living room. Oddly enough, although she had received multiple cuts and bruises, no blood stains were discovered on her beige carpet or, for that matter, anywhere else in her house.

Three suspects were eventually apprehended and indicted for the murder: a young woman and two young men. One suspect, DeWayne Hill, maintained his innocence up to, throughout, and after the trial in which he was convicted as the killer. The other male suspect, Ronnie Martin, was interrogated on September 13, 1989, and admitted that he was in Coon's house with the other two but that the murder was carried out by Hill. Two days later, on September 15, the young woman, Tamesia Russell, was interrogated and confessed to roughly the same thing as Ronnie Martin. Tape recordings were made of both confessions. All three suspects were held at the Richland Parish jail pending trial.

Had the evidence ended here, there may well have been little doubt about the result of Hill's trial despite the absence of any confession from him. Interestingly enough, there is no record of the police even attempting a confession interrogation of Hill. On February 6, 1990, however, Russell was interrogated a second time in response to a motion for suppression of evidence made by her attorney. This interrogation was tape-recorded. Present at this interrogation, in addition to Russell, were the assistant district attorney and Russell's own attorney. At this time, many of the details that Russell had provided in her September 15, 1989, confession were quite different. In addition, she now volunteered that she had lied to her September police interrogator about certain facts because he had threatened her and was trying "to make it hard on her" unless she said some of the things she said.

Later in the same day as the discovery interrogation, February 6, 1990, Russell appeared before the district court judge to plead guilty to one count of robbery and one count of accessory after the fact to murder. This proceeding was not tape-recorded, but a court reporter prepared a transcript of what was purported to be said by all participants. Once again, the details of the evening of the murder were somewhat altered, but the major difference was that Russell now denied that her initial police interrogator had ever made threats or promises to her. She remained in jail until after sentencing, and on December 15, 1990, attorneys for Hill interviewed her once again, tape-recording the proceedings. On this occasion, her story changed drastically once more. Now she claimed that she was never even at the old woman's house, that she had lied to the police, that the interrogating officer had coached her about what to say, and that she was "harassed and threatened" by the police.

Hill's trial for first-degree murder was set, meanwhile, for January 1990. Hill's attorney, Charles Jones of Monroe, had asked me to examine the tape-recorded interrogations and to review the transcripts of Russell's plea hearing to determine whether linguistic analysis of these data might be helpful to Hill at his trial.

One of the most obvious aspects of Russell's four statements was, as noted earlier, their inconsistency across the four statements but even within a given statement. I elected to present these inconsistencies in the form of a chart for the jury to see, organized by the topics in which the inconsistencies occurred. As in the case of Jessie Moffett, the analytical procedure selected was a comparison of the suspect's responses with the same topics that occurred in at least two of the four interrogations in which Russell appeared. Her story varied in 20 topics, as the following chart indicates:

Contradictions in Russell's Statements

Topic	Sept. 15, 1989	Feb. 6, 1990	Feb. 6 1990	Dec. 15, 1990
Tamesia present at murder	Yes (throughout)	Yes (throughout)	Yes (p. 5)	No (p. 1)
Hill and Martin present	Yes (throughout)	Yes (throughout)	Yes (p. 14)	Doesn't know (pp. 4, 5, 7)
Made a block	We did not make a block (p. 9)	We made a block (p. 4) made a block (p. 13) We didn't go make a block (p. 14)		
When she got there	around 1:00 (p. 2)	about 12:30 (p. 3)		Not there at all (pp. 3, 4)
Order of entering	Tamesia first, then Hill and Martin (p. 3)	Tamesia first, then Hill and Martin (pp. 4, 5, 6)	Two men were with her at the time (p. 12)	
Planned robbery	no (p. 9)	They said we was gonna split it (money) 'fore we even went in there (p. 16)	Yes (p. 5)	No. She didn't even go there (p. 1)

Topic	Sept. 15, 1989	Feb. 6, 1990	Feb. 6 1990	Dec. 15, 1990
Whispering	They whispered to each other (all four on the couch) (p. 4) They whispered over Ms. Coon on couch	Hill got up, then Ronnie came out, and they whispered something in each other's ear (p. 8) Ronnie was in the door when they whispered (p. 13)		
Smoked dope	Both of them . . . Caine. (p. 4)	I didn't see no dope (p. 7) I just put in that statement (p. 6) Smoking was a lie (p. 18)		I told him one of those guys. It was a lie (p. 5)
Couch	Hill sat on couch (p. 3) Ronnie sat on couch (p. 4) Ms. Coon in middle (p. 4)	I was sitting in the chair. (p. 2) I sat on couch (p. 6) All four on couch (p. 6) Sat there 10 minutes (p. 7) I was sitting on couch (p. 14)		
Ms. Coon thrown	They put her on the floor . . . just put her on top of the floor . . . she hit the ceiling and then she hit the floor . . . dropped her (p. 5)	He threw her up there and she hit the floor (p. 8) Threw her straight up (p. 8) She fell on the floor (p. 9)		

Topic	Sept. 15, 1989	Feb. 6, 1990	Feb. 6 1990	Dec. 15, 1990
Gray bag/ pouch	gray bag on second couch (p. 7) Martin got change from bag (p. 7) Hill took money from pouch around neck (p. 7)	pouch was gray (p. 16) Ronnie got that (p. 16) It was a little purse thing she had . . . tied around her (p. 9)	She had some tied around her neck (p. 12) Some kind of purse (p. 13) A little pouchlike thing (p. 13) Hill took the money tied around her neck (p. 14)	(The police officer) told her about the pouch (p. 10)
Jar	had a jar (p. 6) didn't see no mayonnaise jar (p. 7) Hill got the jar (p. 7)	There was a mayonnaise jar (p. 16)	money on the floor in a jar (p. 13)	
Amount of money	about $200 (p. 7) jar had change in it (p. 7)	(The police officer) asked me how much it was, and I said about $50 (p. 15)	Some money (p. 6) doesn't know how much (p. 6)	Doesn't recall who she told (The police) took the money It was a lie (p. 11)
Watch	*that* watch was stolen too (p. 7) watch lying by TV (p. 8) Martin got the watch (p. 8)	didn't see anybody take watch (p. 17) (The police officer) brought the watch part up (p. 17)		
Moaning	didn't hear her say anything (p. 8)	She was moaning (p. 9) Q: did she moan? A: No, she didn't say nothing (p. 12)		

Topic	Sept. 15, 1989	Feb. 6, 1990	Feb. 6 1990	Dec. 15, 1990
Fan	a fan was on (p. 8) Martin pointed fan at Ms. Coon's head (p. 8)	fan was running (p. 13)		(The police officer) told her who put the fan on the lady (p. 10) She forgets who she told (the policeman) Lee did it because it was a lie (p. 11)
Porch light	(as they left) Hill turned out the front porch light (p. 8)	She doesn't know if one of them took the light out of the socket (p. 14) didn't see anybody turn out porch light (p. 17) doesn't know whether light was on or off (p. 17)		
Order of leaving	Ronnie, then me, then DeWayne. (p. 8) DeWayne was the last person (p. 8)	I was the first one (pp. 4, 5) Later Hill and Martin left together (p. 6)	all three left together (p. 12)	She wasn't even there (p. 1)
Towel	halfway over her face (p. 6) put towel on her chest (p. 6)	Hill covered her face with towel (p. 9) covered her with towel (p. 10) towel not smothering her (p. 13)		

Topic	Sept. 15, 1989	Feb. 6, 1990	Feb. 6 1990	Dec. 15, 1990
Forced to give statement, threatened	No (p. 11)	told police they smoked dope because was (police) was trying to make it hard on me (p. 7) (The police officer) said if I didn't say something I would end up in the electric chair (p. 12) They threatening, telling me I was going to get the electric chair (p. 12)	no one made threats or promises (p. 10)	(six statements)

From this chart, it is immediately apparent that Tamesia Russell simply had a terrible memory, that she was a very amateurish liar, that she was afraid of her interlocutor, or that she knowingly changed her story with great regularity for some unknown purpose. The problem is which version of her story, if any, can we believe? It would be tempting to say that Russell told the officer at her initial interrogation on September 15, 1989, whatever he apparently wanted to hear. If this is the case, then it could also be true that she told Hill's attorneys whatever they wanted to hear on December 15, 1990. But why, then, did she alter her story and admit to lying to the police in her February 6, 1990, interrogation with the assistant district attorney and her own lawyer? And why did she alter it again in her court appearance later that same day? The accommodation theory of lying does not seem to fit Tamesia Russell. She is quite capable of disagreeing with her interrogator. In her December 15, 1990, interview with Hill's attorney, for example, the following exchange is illustrative:

Jones: You knew that you were gonna get 12 years after you got through talking, didn't you?

Russell: Not really. He said it couldn't be not more than like around 7 to 12.

If Russell were simply accommodating to everything she believed Hill's attorney wanted to hear, she certainly didn't do so here.

Being able to disagree with an interlocutor is one bit of evidence of lack of fear of that individual. Another kind of evidence comes from her length of utterance. In her initial interrogation by the police officer (September 15, 1989), 53% of her utterances were the 1-word type. In her police interrogation, only 8% of her responses were 10 or more words long, whereas in her interview with Hill's attorney, 15% were 10 words or more. The correlation of brevity with fear seems apparent here.

It was not difficult to piece together other evidence that Russell was afraid of the police interrogator. I have already noted that she admitted to the assistant district attorney on February 6, 1990, that the police had threatened her. The tape recording of that interrogation, however, contains no evidence of such threats. It is inconceivable, however, that the tape recording of December 15, 1989, includes everything that both Russell and the police officer ever said to each other. The tape recorder was apparently turned on long after the interview had started. The tape itself gives evidence of a preceding conversation, as the following quotations indicate:

Evidence That the Police Officer Had
Talked With Russell Before Taping

---

1. p. 3   Q: And *you said* another individual came in. What was his name?
         A: Ronnie Martin.

         . . .

         Q: OK, and how did *they* get into the house?
         A: *They* knocked, and she opened the door.
2. p. 3   Q: OK, in relation to where you were sitting, would DeWayne have been sitting on *the end of the couch by you* or on the end of the couch by the TV?
3. p. 4   Q: OK, and, uh, you mentioned *before going on tape* that somebody smoked some drugs.
4. p. 5   Q: OK, what was he going through, do you know?
         A: Purse.
         Q: Can you describe some of *these purses*?
5. p. 5   Q: Where were you?
         A: Still in *the* chair.

6. p. 7 Q: OK. And, uh, do you remember seeing any other money in Mrs. Coon's house?

A: No. Besides what they got out of *that* jar

7. p. 7 Q: OK, did, *going back to the pouch* that was around her neck *that you mentioned* that DeWayne Hill took from her.

8. p. 7 Q: OK, and what else was taken from her residence?

A: Nothing besides the money and *that* watch.

Q: Where was *that* watch located?

In Quotes 1, 3, and 7, the police officer directly refers to a preceding conversation with Russell ("you said," "you mentioned before going on tape," "that you mentioned"). The police officer's referencing system also makes clear that certain topics had been discussed earlier, as Quotes 1, 5, 6, and 8 make clear. At the point at which the police officer says, ". . . how did *they* get into the house," reference had been made to only one other person, Ronnie Martin. When Russell answers the question "Where were you?" with "Still in *the* chair," her use of the word *the* reveals that she had spoken about a specific chair earlier. Otherwise, she would have said *a* chair. Similarly, Russell's use of the demonstrative *that* in Quotes 6 and 8 ("that jar" and "that watch") gives evidence that these topics had been discussed before.

Because of such clear evidence that considerable conversation had taken place between the police officer and Russell before the tape recorder was activated, we can assume that the threatening that Russell speaks about in her February 6 and December 15, 1990, interrogations must have occurred at that period of time.

The bad memory theory is unconvincing because there is no evidence of a unidirectional decline over time in her ability to retain details. Some facts get added over time, and others change even within the same interview. Perhaps she had some clever plan in mind to convince her interrogators of her innocence by creating the ludicrous contradictions that her four interrogations reveal. If so, it was either not very clever after all or so ingenious that nobody ever figured it out. For what it is worth, she appeared as a prosecution witness at Hill's murder trial. Her story at that time was closest to the one she gave the police in her first interrogation on September 15, 1989.

My chart of inconsistencies across the four interrogations of Tamesia Russell ends with the topic of threatening. The six times that Russell said she was threatened in her December 15, 1990, interview were the focus of my next chart.

Russell Says She Was Threatened, December 15, 1990

---

p. 1   I was being harassed and threatened by Willie Lee Robinson. . . . He was saying that if I didn't say something about the case, I be like get the chair, couldn't see my mother no more. I'd get life in the penitentiary.

p. 2   Q: The only reason that you made that statement saying that was because they had told you that you were gonna die?

     A: Yes sir.

p. 5   Q: But why did you tell him that DeWayne Hill and Ronnie Martin was smoking dope?

     A: Um huh-uh (I don't know)

     Q: Did you tell him that because he *threatened* you and you were afraid?

     A: Yeah. He had been threatening me ever since I got picked up from where I was at.

p. 5   Q: Did you tell (the assistant district attorney) that these people had threatened you and that you were afraid and that is why you gave this statement?

     A: Yeah. And I told my lawyer too.

p. 6   Q: You mean you told your lawyer . . . about (the police officer) threatening you and electric chair and all of that?

     A: Yes sir.

p. 6   Q: And that's why he (your lawyer) filed this Motion to Suppress your confession was because you had told him that you didn't—you weren't there, you didn't know anything about no murder and that these people had, (the police officer) had threatened you, right?

     A: Yes.

Another speech act that occurs regularly in Russell's four statements is that of admitting, in this case admitting that she had lied. The following chart displays these instances.

Russell Directly Admits Lying, February 6, 1990

---

p. 6   Assistant D.A.:   You stated earlier that DeWayne and Ronnie smoked some dope while they were in the house. Did they do that?

     Russell: No, Ma'am. I just put that in the statement.

p. 7   Assistant D.A.:   . . . why did you tell the police that they smoked some dope inside the house?

     Russell: 'Cause they was trying to make it hard on me so (inaudible)

p. 15	Assistant D.A.:	Tamesia, you told the police that DeWayne got about $200 out of the pouch.
	Russell:	I don't know exactly how much it was but, what I said, Willie Lee ask me how much it was, and I said about $50, and Willie Lee said, you sure it wasn't more than that, about $200 or something? And I just said yeah.
p. 17	Assistant D.A.:	OK, you also mentioned that she had a watch. Did Miss Coon have a watch?
	Russell:	I don't really know 'cause Willie Lee brought the watch part up.
	Assistant D.A.:	OK, so you didn't see anybody take a watch.
	Russell:	No.
p. 18	Assistant D.A.:	You said earlier that you kinda made up some things when Willie was talking to you.
p. 4	Assistant D.A.:	So everything in this statement that we are talking about (September 15, 1989) is not the truth. Is that correct?
	Russell:	Yes sir.
p. 5	Russell:	I told him one of the guys (smoked dope). . . It was a lie.
p. 7	Assistant D.A.:	You mean everything in that statement is not the truth?
	Russell:	Everything.
p. 7	Assistant D.A.:	Why did you lie to her (the assistant D.A.)?
	Russell:	I told her I wasn't there from the jump. She should of knowed then.
pp. 7-8	Assistant D.A.:	So everything that you said in your statement except your name and address and all on February 6th, that's no truth in any of that statement. Is that correct?
	Russell:	Yes.
p. 11	Assistant D.A.:	OK, you don't even remember who you told him put the fan on the lady do you?
	Russell:	Huh-uh.
	Assistant D.A.:	Why, why don't you remember?
	Russell:	'Cause it was a lie.
p. 11	Assistant D.A.:	So none of this is true except your name and your address, is that correct?
	Russell:	Yes.
p. 11	Assistant D.A.:	Well, why did you lie to the judge . . .
	Russell:	I done told you. I was scared.

Not all evidence of Russell's lying are as explicit and direct as the above. After explaining language indirectness briefly, I offered the following examples from her December 15, 1990, interview:

Russell Indirectly Admits to Lying, December 15, 1990

---

p. 2	Q:	Did you make a statement to him?
	A:	Yes sir.
	Q:	And in that statement you said you were there?
	A:	Yes sir.
	Q:	And, uh, but you weren't there
	A:	No, Sir.
	Q:	You weren't at the house at all?
	A:	No, Sir.
p. 3	Q:	And then you said what he told you to say?
	A:	Yes sir.
p. 3	Q:	Because you weren't even there, were you?
	A:	No, Sir.
p. 4	Q:	But none of that was true because Ronnie Martin didn't come, did he?
	A:	No.
p. 4	Q:	DeWayne never was there to even sit on the couch, did he?
	A:	If he wasn't there, he couldn't sit.
	Q:	Why did you say that?
	A:	'Cause he told me to say it.

When persons are caught in a lie or when they openly admit to lying, the obvious next question is, Why did you tell the lie? Liars can respond in several ways: They can mutter something about mere forgetfulness, attempting to trivialize the event. They can blame it on someone else, as Russell did when she explained that the police officer had threatened and harassed her. Another way to shift the responsibility for lying is to claim that she lied because someone else told her what to say, coached her, or scripted her testimony. Russell did exactly this in both her February 6, 1990, and December 15, 1990, statements, as the following indicates:

Russell Says the Police Officer Told
Her What to Say, February 6, 1990

---

p. 12	Q:	You gave a statement to the police on September 15, last year. Was that statement voluntary? Did they make you give that statement?

A: Well, in a way, 'cause (the officer), when they come pick me up, he kept on, I kept on telling them, and then he said if I don't say something, I would end up in the electric chair.

p. 15 Q: Tamesia, you told the police that DeWayne got about $200 out of the pouch.

A: I don't know exactly how much it was, but what I said, (the police officer) ask me how much it was, and I said "about $50," and (he) said, "You sure it wasn't more than that, about $200 or something?" and I just said, "Yeah."

p. 17 Q: OK, you also mentioned that she had a watch. Did Miss Coon have a watch?

A: I don't really exactly know 'cause (the police officer) brought the watch part up.

p. 18 Q: You said earlier that you kinda made up some things when (the officer) was talking to you.

A: Only thing I put in was the part about smoking.

p. 1 Q: Did he tell you what to say?

A: Yeah, in so many words he told me.

p. 2 Q: . . . he asked you to pretty much say back to him what he read to you?

A: Yes sir.

p. 3 Q: Did he pretty much kinda tell you what to say?

A: Yes sir.

Q: OK. He told you what to say in this case?

A: Yes sir.

Q: OK. And then you said what he told you to say?

A: Yes sir.

p. 3 Q: Now before you gave that statement you started talking about 1:00 o'clock that night on Wednesday morning—had he told you what to say and the time you were supposed to have been there and all that kind of stuff?

A: Yeah. 'Cause I didn't know.

p. 8 Q: So during the Boykin . . . they had already agreed that the maximum that you were gonna get would be 12 years. They had told you that, didn't they?

A: Yeah.

Q: So they told you, look if you go on and plead guilty to this, the maximum time that you are gonna get is 12 years and, uh, you knew that before you even went into court that day, didn't you?

A: Yeah.

Q: They told you, though, that you had to admit doing something in order to get this 12 years, didn't they?

A: Yes sir.

Q: Who told you that?

A: (The police officer) was the one that told me, that's all.

p. 9 Q: Did he (the officer) go over any of these statements with you before you went in on your Boykin hearing? He sit down and go over them with you and tell you what to tell the judge?

A: He sat down and talked to me about some—what was on paper. I wasn't really into it 'cause I ain't knowed nothing. I been talking about what he was telling me to do.

To this point, the focus of my analysis was on the four conflicting and fluid statements of the major witness against DeWayne Hill, Tamesia Russell, largely because her words provide a goldmine of evidence for Hill's defense. What jury could believe a person who so readily admits to lying and who changes her story each time she talks on the record? But there was another witness as well, Ronnie Martin. Martin gave only one statement, on September 13, 1989. The prosecution did not permit him to speak under oath afterward. His one statement was not nearly as dramatically inconsistent as Russell's, and it posed the problem of how to address it. One obvious answer was to compare Martin's statements with Russell's on whatever similar topics both addressed. I chose to compare his statements on these topics with Russell's at the same time frame, mid-September, 1989, to ensure comparability. Even then, 10 mutually discussed topics displayed factual differences, as the following chart indicates:

Contradictions: Martin and Russell Statements, September, 1989

Topic		Martin September 13		Russell September 15
Who was with whom	p. 2	DeWayne and Tamesia together. They asked me did I want to make a little money. DeWayne asked first.	p. 9	I's walking by myself
Reason for going there	p. 2	They asked me did I want to make a little money.	p. 9	She had lights on, and she don't usually have her light on.
Order of entering	p. 3	1. Tamesia 2. DeWayne 3. Ronnie	p. 3	1. Tamesia, 2. two men together
Dope	p. 2	Tamesia asked me did I have a shooter (for caine)	p. 4	Both of 'em (shraked) . . . caine
Made a block	p. 3	We made a whole block	p. 9	we did not make a block
Porch light	p. 3	One of them turned that porch light off before we got in	p. 8	Hill turned out the front porch light (as they left)
Sitting on couch	p. 3	Tamesia, Ms. Coon, DeWayne	p. 4	Ronnie, Ms. Coon, DeWayne

Topic		Martin September 13		Russell September 15
Ceiling	p. 5	didn't notice ceiling, plaster on floor.	p. 5	Ceiling cracked and scattered on floor
Order of leaving	p. 5	Tamesia and DeWayne first, then Ronnie	p. 8	Ronnie, then me, then DeWayne
Direction of leaving	p. 5	DeWayne and Tamesia went toward Jessie's stand. I went another way—by funeral home	p. 8	I went straight up front toward church. I seen DeWayne go behind that back way with Ronnie.

What we have here, then, is a case of *implicational confession,* both by Tamesia Russell and by Ronnie Martin. They both confess to robbing Ms. Coon and to being an accessory to her murder, but they confess the murder on behalf of DeWayne Hill because he never personally confessed to anything and was never asked to. The state used the conventional approach to the case, starting with the little guys to get to the alleged main player, the actual murderer. The fact that Martin's and Russell's stories were inconsistent with each other and, in Russell's case, even internally inconsistent made the state's job considerably more complicated.

Because of the many glaring inconsistencies in reporting details, because of so much clear evidence of lying, and because of ample evidence to believe that the police threatened and harassed Russell, the felicity of these implicational confessions could be challenged. If Martin and Russell were confessing to the lesser charges of robbery and accessory, one is led to wonder why they were doing so. If we can believe what Russell said to Hill's attorney on December 15, 1990, she confessed to robbery and accessory because she was convinced by the police interrogator that unless she did this she probably would have been convicted of first-degree murder. Although the prosecution protected Martin from any further interviews, it is possible that he had the same fears. Both Russell and Martin had police records. Hill did not. Both Russell and Martin were known to have used drugs. Hill was not. The three knew each other, but not well.

The defense attorney for DeWayne Hill firmly believed that his client did not commit the murder and that his involvement was a creation of Martin and Russell to reduce the charges made against them. For reasons unclear to the defense attorneys, the jury convicted DeWayne Hill after a very brief deliberation. Apparently, they believed the testimony of Tamesia Russell, who repeated under oath most of her original story to the police interrogator.

Language of the Interrogator as Therapist

Researchers have been puzzled about why a police interrogation can cause innocent people to incriminate themselves (or appear to do so). A coerced confession is one answer, but laws against coercion are very clear, at least about physical coercion, making promises of lenience, and threatening the suspect. But the law does not deal with subtler forms of coercion, such as pretending to be sympathetic to the suspect, even to the extent of being his or her trusted ally. Whether within the law or not, such techniques are what they are, simple coercion.

Kassin's (1995) research on coercion, noted in Chapter 2, points out that subtle coercive approaches can be just as influential on suspects as the more blatant, illegal kind. Wrightsman and Kassin (1993, pp. 86-93) describe three kinds of false confession: (a) voluntary (no external pressure), (b) coerced-compliant (an innocent person confesses to avoid an adverse situation or to achieve approval), and (c) coerced-internalized (a suspect becomes convinced that he or she is guilty). It is not surprising that most people find it difficult to believe that a coerced-compliant or coerced-internalized confession is actually false.

Another answer to why people give false confessions may be found in what Foster (1969) calls the *stationhouse syndrome:* "police interrogation . . . can produce a trance-like state of heightened suggestibility" (p. 690). Wrightsman and Kassin (1993) observe that the hypnotic state is, in its extreme, the essence of suggestibility (p. 94). Gudjonsson and Clark (1986) developed the concept of *interrogative suggestibility* and noted that the interrogator can manipulate uncertainty, interpersonal trust, and expectation to change the suspect's susceptibility to suggestions (p. 282) (For an excellent review of the research on this topic, see Wrightsman & Kassin, 1993).

► Persuasion of Beverly Monroe

A classic example of a police investigator attempting to create either a coerced-compliant or coerced-internalized confession taking is found in the case of *Commonwealth of Virginia v. Beverly A. Monroe,* which came to trial in October 1992. Monroe was a 54-year-old white female charged with the homicide of Roger de la Burde, whose body was found on March 5, 1992, on the floor of his home in Powhatan County, Virginia. Monroe had dined with Burde the previous evening at his home. She claims she left Burde's home at about 9:30 p.m., went to her own home, came back the next morning, and found Burde dead with one bullet shot to his head.

Monroe gave her initial statement to Deputy Sheriff Neal on the day the body was discovered. Some 3 weeks later, State Police Officer David Riley began his investigation of the case and met with Monroe. He asked her to take a lie detector test. She agreed but allegedly failed two questions: "Were you present when he was shot?" and "Did you shoot him?" She answered no to both of these questions, and the polygraph examiner concluded that she had given untruthful answers.

On March 26, Riley confronted Monroe with the findings of the polygraph on these two questions but took a sympathetic position toward her. He told her there must be some explanation for this result. He went into great detail about how familiar he was with suicide because his own father had committed suicide, and he told Monroe that he was aware that her father, too, had committed suicide. He explained that people often go into shock after such a traumatic event, blocking out all memory of it. He suggested that she must have been present when Burde shot himself but that she had managed to obliterate this from her memory. He said he was satisfied that this was a case of suicide but that she must have been present.

Throughout the tape-recorded conversations that Riley conducted with Monroe, his stance is that of a sympathetic friend, trying always to get information that would confirm that Burde died by his own hand. He placed Monroe in the position of a key to helping verify this scenario if only she could regain her memory of the event. At no point does Riley lead Monroe to believe that she is a suspect in the case.

Monroe's attorney, Murray Janus, asked me to analyze the tape-recorded conversations, which were to be the basis of the charge of murder against Beverly Monroe. The tapes were of rather poor quality acoustically. Riley's voice was usually clear enough, but Monroe's speech was very low and often inaudible. Nevertheless, several careful listenings on high-quality equipment enabled me to produce a transcript with most of the dialogue revealed.

Riley's first meeting with Monroe, on March 26, immediately followed the polygraph exam, which was also tape-recorded. At the conclusion of the polygraph test, we hear Riley's voice saying, "I'm gonna go out and make a few notes and write a few questions down. Then when I come back, we'll get this over with." The tape is then shut off. When the tape is turned back on, Monroe is speaking in midsentence about her father. It is not possible to know how much conversation took place before Riley started the tape recorder, but it is clear that there was some. Monroe had mentioned in her polygraph test that Burde had a gun at his house and that she remembered seeing it that night. Because a note was found by the body, Riley asked her whether she had seen the note. She responds, "No, no." At this point, Riley begins a series of suggestions that she had actually blocked out important facts:

DR: All you saw was the gun?

BM: That's right.

DR: You saw the gun, and you remembered the notes.

BM: I have this vision (unintelligible) like that.

DR: You have the vision, you remember lying on the couch. You remember seeing the gun.

BM: I remember seeing the gun.

DR: You remember seeing the gun, and then you remember that you were home, you had this unconscious feeling that something was wrong. You couldn't remember what. And you made the calls. And you, somehow I was surprised when the phone didn't, didn't, when he didn't answer the phone.

BM: That really bothered me.

DR: And then, but something in your mind, because you remember what you saw in the back of your mind, seein' him on the couch. You remember seeing him there, and all night long, all you wanted to do was go to him and be with him and see that he was found, and it just ate at you all night long . . . It's something eatin' you right now. Beverly, you're gonna sleep better, you'll sleep better if you remember this. You'll sleep better.

BM: I'm gonna try.

DR: Tell me again.

BM: I'd like to be able to see.

DR: Tell me again, look at, just look through me right now. Look through me right now and tell me again. You hear the noise, you're asleep or you're in a sleepy state. You're on your couch. You remember jumping and standing and seeing a gun . . . you remember standing over him and seeing the gun, and you remember leaving the house and making the phone calls. And you remember leavin' him asleep on the couch . . . but you know now he didn't walk you to the door. But that's what he always did before. But you know now that's not true. You know that he didn't really walk you to the door because you left him asleep on the couch.

BM: This vision of him, some other time—

DR: Yeah, but you left him asleep on the couch. And you remember lookin' down and seein' that gun. And you just couldn't face it. You could not face tellin' people, callin' them and sayin' I was here when this thing happened. It was just, just too much for you to deal with at that moment. And it was just overwhelming.

BM: That's a hard thing to understand.

DR: No, no it's not. It's hard to admit, sure, but it's not hard to understand.

Riley's tactic of planting the seed that Monroe had actually witnessed Burde's suicide was repeated throughout his conversations with her. His approach had at its basis the common tactic of getting a suspect to admit less important facts as a wedge to the crucial ones. If Riley could get Monroe to admit she was actually present at Burde's suicide, the next step would be to connect her to the murder. What he had to go on for this was the results of the polygraph test, his knowledge that persons who discover the body are often the perpetrators, his knowledge that Monroe was aware that Burde had been unfaithful to her, and her inconsistent statement first that Burde had walked her to the door when she left and then that she had left him asleep on his couch. If he could only get Monroe to admit she was present at Burde's death, he thought, he could take her to the next step of confession to the murder. Riley gave every evidence of being convinced that he had actually gotten Monroe to believe she was, indeed, present at Burde's suicide. Her voice on the tape was often muddy and unclear, leading the prosecution to accept Riley's conclusion because they could not really hear her words.

The question for linguistic analysis was, Did Monroe ever adopt Riley's suggestion? The approach to finding the answer was first to isolate the substantive topics of Riley through a conventional topic analysis and then to carry out a response analysis of Monroe's reactions to Riley's topics. Such an analysis aids the jury by first finding and categorizing all crucial passages. By "crucial passages," I mean those on which both the prosecution's case and the defense's case are based. Such analysis is bound neither to the need to prosecute nor the need to defend. It simply isolates and categorizes what was on the tape.

It was apparent that the prosecution firmly agreed with Riley that Monroe had actually confessed to being at the suicide scene. But the prosecution offered no transcript of the tapes as an aid to the jury, a tactic I found unusual because when the prosecution believes that the tape-recorded evidence is incriminating, it does not hesitate to commit the spoken word to paper. Jurors, like anyone else, are convinced by what they hear, but they remember better what they see. Thus, it is useful for the prosecution to play the tapes to convince the jury about what they contain, but it is equally useful to keep such information before the jury and fixed in their memory by giving them a transcript. In this trial, no such transcript was offered, so I made my own.

During the process of preparing a transcript, I began to realize why the prosecution had not made its own. Unless the prosecution got technical help, such a transcript would have contained so little speech by Monroe as to appear ludicrous. Riley completely dominated these conversations in quantity of talk. When Monroe does try to say something, she is usually interrupted midsentence by Riley. Monroe's voice is very low and frequently inaudible, causing still further difficulty to any effort by the prosecution to prepare an accurate transcript. It appeared most obvious, however, once I had pulled out all the speech that was possible to understand, that Riley's statements are often unrelated to what Monroe is saying. It appears that he paid little attention to her contributions and plowed right on with his own agenda.

By preparing a transcript of these conversations, the government would highlight the weaknesses of the police officer as a finder of facts. Instead, it would reveal an investigator who is single-minded in his goal, rather than open, nonresponsive to his subject's answers and comments, suggestive to the extent of appearing to mesmerize or hypnotize the subject, and more concerned with persuasion and trickery than with discovering what had actually occurred. Such a picture would not be attractive to a jury.

In my testimony at trial, I produced charts of Riley's five major, recurring topics:

1. You left him dead
2. You're not telling the truth
3. You saw the gun
4. You left Burde's house earlier than you said you did
5. You were there when it happened

I charted Monroe's responses next to each of Riley's taped quotations under each topic, thus presenting a topic analysis and a response analysis at the same time.

Topic: You Left Him Dead

This topic of Detective Riley was, in essence, an accusation. It is permissible for interrogators to accuse suspects, but Riley was faced with the difficult task of accusing while at the same time appearing to be on Monroe's side. His strategy, therefore, had to be accomplished carefully, so he couched it in terms of Monroe's fragile emotional state, having deep feelings about her own father's suicide, which apparently caused her to obliterate from memory her presence at Burde's death. His tone of voice was tender, and he took her perspective to the extent of using first-person pronouns to represent what he believed she was thinking. Riley also cleverly attempted to convert certain of Monroe's actions into something quite different, as the following exchange indicates:

Riley	*Monroe*
p. 3 And all night long, all you wanted to do was go to him and be with him and see that he was found, and it just ate at you all night long.	It's something I (unintelligible)—

Here, Riley builds on Monroe's concern for Burde, having left him that night in a somewhat melancholy state. When she got home, she tried to telephone him but got no answer. She knew he often turned his telephone off in the evening, but she admitted to being concerned about him anyway. The key word in Riley's statement is *found*. If Monroe knew Burde was dead, his being found would make sense, so Riley converts her concern to that of leaving Burde's body unattended. Monroe's response gives no clear indication of how she perceived Riley's statement because two or three syllables were unintelligible, but there is no way to interpret her response as an adoption of Riley's suggestion. The remaining examples of Riley's topic You Left Him Dead are the following:

You Left Him Dead

	Riley	Monroe
p. 8	You thought, what a horrible person I am because I have left him without somebody to take care of him. . . That's the worst thing, isn't it?	I think so.
p. 9	And then all night long you said I've left him, I've left him like that, I can't stand the idea that I've left him like that. I've got to see that he's taken care of. And you could not go anywhere until you found, made sure that he was taken care of.	It wasn't a conscious move. It's just, when I started to go to work, I had (unintelligible)—
p. 10	. . . He was gone. You wanted to see that his remains were taken care of. The last thing you could do for him, to be sure that he didn't lay there all day long . . . you couldn't stand the thought of him being there all day long . . . not knowing when somebody would find him	(unintelligible) consciousness. I just (unintelligible)
	. . . I know the thought. I've lost people, and I know that I couldn't have stood the thought 'til somebody found him	Yeah. That's why I had to go I—
	Had to find him	'Cause I tried to and I couldn't—
p. 15	You knew in your dream, all night long that this thing was eatin' at you, I left Roger there, I can't, the family is just not going to understand this because I've left him there. And you had to get him found . . . you couldn't count on when somebody would find him. You didn't want him . . . to be left there for a day or two days. You know that. Did you?	I don't remember . . . saying anything like that
	But you—	Just (unintelligible) I really mean it
	. . . and you wanted someone to find him so in your unconscious you're still tryin' to believe that it didn't happen	I'm tryin' not to believe—
	I know. But believe it.	

	Riley	Monroe
p. 17	And you saw him, you heard the noise, you saw him . . . you could not deal with it at the moment. You left and you went home, made two calls, thought about him there all night long.	(unintelligible) called him.
	Yes, you did.	(unintelligible) wouldn't answer.
	No, you didn't. You *hoped* he would answer. . . You didn't think he would answer.	

Notice that Riley does not let up on his theme, trying to convince Monroe to remember that her boyfriend was dead when she left him. Although Monroe's responses are sometimes inaudible, it is clear that she holds to her position that she has no such memory and does not adopt Riley's hypothesis.

Topic: You're Not Telling the Truth

It is acceptable within the law for police interrogators to accuse subjects of the suspected crimes and to accuse them of lying. Riley's task is a touchy one here because he is trying to cause Monroe to believe that he is her friend and counselor while, at the same time, accusing her of lying without destroying that friendship.

Riley's first strategy to avoid losing his role as counselor and friend is to appear to stand in Monroe's shoes. He does this by shifting his description of his hypothetical scenario to the first person, as follows:

	Riley	Monroe
p. 6	I'm not tellin' the truth. Why is that that this is not why—	(unintelligible)—
	And I'm not telling the truth. What is it that I know that keeps me from tellin' the truth?	(unintelligible) saying to myself (unintelligible)
	So I'm not tellin' this man the truth.	(unintelligible)
	So I knew in my mind, my mind says one thing, but my heart's saying something else.	(unintelligible)

Riley	Monroe
I know it. And that's how it works.	And I couldn't understand why these feelings were coming (unintelligible) That's the kind I had in the car. Sometimes I (unintelligible) makes me jump. I just jump. . . . I mean it (unintelligible) and I don't know exactly where it comes from.

Riley avoids saying "You're lying" by switching the pronoun to *I*. This tactic has two advantages: (a) It avoids the appearance of the I-accuse-you speech act (even though it maintains the substance of it) and (b) it joins Monroe and Riley as a merged entity. This difficult situation is thereby alleged not to be "I" against "you," but rather "we" against some unspecified opponent (perhaps memory) best characterized as "it" or "them." Nevertheless, Monroe does not adopt Riley's position fully. She admits to having uneasy feelings when she left Burde and that she continues to be jumpy—not surprising, considering that her lover has just experienced a violent death—but she says she doesn't know exactly where the feelings come from. This statement leaves the door slightly open for Riley to continue, and he next escalates his accusation of lying, as follows:

Accuse of Lying

	Riley	Monroe
p. 10	You've known all along there was something that you haven't told us that you felt, that's made you feel guilty, had a guilty feeling about something.	That's not true.
p. 15	But you know, now that you've talked to me, what happened, don't you? You might not want to accept it consciously, but you know, from talking to me, what happened, don't you? Give me that much.	OK.
	You know that, don't you? Tell me yes.	Yes, I guess so. I didn't really (unintelligible)—
	You do know this.	I wish I could see it.
	You can see it. . . . You still havin' a hard time?	Yeah, some things—
	You still havin' a hard time describing it, but you see it. (changes subject)	

Riley	Monroe
p. 17 You know what I've told you's true. You know it, don't you?	I can't, I wish I could see it.
You can see it. You'll see it. You'll see it. You'll see it in your dreams, and eventually you'll remember.	

Having previously gotten Monroe to admit that something is bothering her even though she does not admit to lying, Riley identifies these feelings as guilt. Monroe denies this as well. Undaunted, Riley then adopts the authority father role, "But you know, now that you've talked to me," as an appeal to Monroe that she "knows" what happened, even scripting her desired response, "Tell me yes." Monroe has a hard time disagreeing with Riley's authority, first yielding an inch with, "Yes, I guess so," and then backing off with, "I wish I could see it." The latter response, though not adopting Riley's suggestion, at least offers him hope of a compliant subject. She says she wants to agree with him even though she isn't yet able to. On page 17, Riley recycles his authority, Monroe repeats her "I don't adopt, but I'm willing to adopt" stance, and Riley concludes by saying, in effect, you'll see it and remember it eventually:

Riley	Monroe
p. 3 . . . Look through me right now and tell me again. You hear the noise, you're asleep . . . you're on the couch. You remember jumping and standing and seeing the gun.	I'd like to be able to see it.
p. 4 But you remember standing over him and seeing the gun . . . and you remember leavin' him asleep on the couch.	I don't know how it got there.

Topic: You Saw the Gun

Monroe stated earlier that she had seen a gun at Burde's house. Riley's self-imposed task was to get Monroe to remember, believe, or at least say that she remembers seeing the gun in Burde's hand at the time of the shooting. Such an admission would, of course, place her at the death scene, a necessary first step for a murder confession. He begins by trying to pinpoint where and when Monroe saw the gun, as follows:

Saw Gun

	Riley	Monroe
p. 4	But you left him asleep on the couch. And you remember lookin' down and seein' that gun. And you just couldn't face it. You could not face tellin' people, callin' them and sayin' I was here when this thing happened. . .	. . . That's a hard thing to understand
p. 50	And then you'd have these flashes. You'd see that gun in his hand. You'd have these flashes all night long, seein' that gun in his hand.	I don't remember. In fact, I've had them since (unintelligible). I can't see a sound (sigh). It just makes me jump.
	You heard the sound, though. You told me a while ago you heard the sound. . . .	I know when it comes to me—
	Don't let it go away from you. Don't rationalize it away. Don't do that.	I won't. I won't.
	Some do that. But you know . . . that that man didn't lie to you.	I have to feel it myself—
p. 6	You were on the couch. Something made you jump. You remember at some point after that you looked down at Roger and you saw the gun and you realized what happened. Maybe your unconscious mind doesn't remember that, but your unconscious mind remembers it, and that's what you're tellin' me.	(unintelligible) in my mind—
p. 11	That's because you remember in your subconscious seein' the gun. You remember lookin' there. You remember hearin' the noise.	I know I (unintelligible) (sigh)
	And you looked for that. You told me a minute ago that you're—	But I'm just—
	No, you looked.	I looked for something—
	You looked, you looked that night when this happened, you looked. There's got to be some, whenever at some point, conscious or unconscious, Roger, what did you tell me? What did you tell me? Did you look for something? And you couldn't find it. Or maybe you did.	Huh-uh

Riley	Monroe
Nothing?	No, 'cause it was actually later when I looked in the, in the—
(changes subject) What time did you think you really left?	

Of particular interest here is Monroe's non-adoption of Riley's suggestions. She does not remember, she can't see it, she has to feel it herself. Her responses then become more and more inaudible, making it difficult to tell whether her words indicate disagreement. But we can know that she was disagreeing, or at least non-adopting, from Riley's responses to her statements. His "that's because" statement on page 11 signals that she has said something that does not comport with Riley's theory. He outright disagrees with what Monroe said with his, "No, you looked."

It is noteworthy here that Riley interrupts Monroe's attempts to produce statements contrary to his theory at least six times on this topic, finally changing the subject completely. Such interruptive behavior is consistent with the interrogator's trying to control the entire conversation toward his own goals. Conversation sometimes is like a football game, with an offense and a defense. The offense tries to score, and the defense tries to prevent the other team from accomplishing its aims. One way to block the other team is to cause it to fumble the ball. Interruption reflects such an effort.

Topic: You Left Burde's House
Later Than You Said You Did

If Riley can catch Monroe in a lie, even a minor one, he has a wedge to use against her argument that she knew nothing about Burde's death. In her earlier statement, Monroe estimated that she left Burde's house at about 9:20 p.m. Monroe's son was home when she arrived, but he made no particular note of his mother's arrival time, not considering it important. Therefore, his testimony was not especially useful to the defense. Unlike the preceding accusations, Riley can be a bit more forceful with this topic because Monroe's time of departure seemed inconsequential and his disagreement would do little or no damage to his perceived role as therapist/friend. Therefore, he is more direct and forceful, contradicting Monroe vigorously, as follows:

Accuses of Leaving Later

Riley	Monroe
p. 12 You didn't leave that early. I know you didn't leave that early. I know. Something tells me. I know something that—	But (unintelligible)
I know something—	(unintelligible)
. . . you didn't leave at 9:20. You left later than that . . . maybe an hour or so later.	But how can you know that?
I do. I know that. Because Roger made a phone call . . . probably while you were asleep.	to Don (unintelligible)?
You remember?	Don told me.
Yeah, and you were asleep . . . you had to be there when he made the call.	(unintelligible)
But there are phones all over the house. He made the call probably down the hall.	Well, that's true.

To this accusation, Monroe remains politely firm. She does not appear to accept Riley's claim to omniscience ("Something tells me") and his claim to "know" this to be true. She challenges, "But how can you know that?" Riley then reveals his trump card, his knowledge that Roger Burde made a telephone call during the period that he believes Monroe was still at Burde's house. But Monroe had learned this from another source, the man who made the call. Riley then tries to rehabilitate his theory by saying that because there were telephones all over the house, Monroe may not have heard this call even though she was there. Monroe's response, "Well, that's true," can only mean that she is aware of the fact that the house had many telephones.

Topic: You Were There When It Happened

The day following this interrogation, Riley engaged Monroe in a long tape-recorded telephone conversation. The most significant aspect of this call is that Riley now takes the stance that they had reached agreement in the preceding interrogation that she was, indeed, present at the death of her lover. Nothing in Monroe's language could lead him to such a conclusion. Nevertheless, he now makes statements such as, ". . . you now realize you were there," and, ". . . we resolved one issue yesterday," and, ". . . you can tell Corrina the same way that you told me," as the following indicates:

Accuses of Being There

	Riley	Monroe
pp. 1, 2		I'm at the office. I had to come in this morning to work on things that are just piling up to the (unintelligible) You have this sense of great responsibility—
	Especially since you now realize you were there. Well. It, it—	It doesn't come to my mind. I can't bring it to my vision.
p. 6	Well, look. We resolved one issue yesterday, and that was the only thing accounted for. Resolved issue was that the reason that, that your behavior was so strange and, and inappropriate and even though you didn't realize it at the time . . . had to do with the fact that you were present. . . . we got that out in the interview. . . . That issue has been resolved . . .	I don't understand that, and that's (unintelligible)—. . . but I really need to, I, I'm not the kind of person to see in black and white because, you know, I just couldn't.
p. 7	Well, you mean you don't feel like you can tell Corrina the same way you told me?	Have to think about it . . . but I have to tell her I feel responsible.
p. 10	Beverly, you answered my questions yesterday.	Did I?
	Yes, I mean—	I don't know (unintelligible) my own, yet.
p. 10	. . . There was some things that you did and said, and quite frankly I don't think you were really conscious of what you did and said—	Not (unintelligible) because I don't—
p. 11	. . . it's always the one in your mind that when, if you're there or present or close by—	I really don't know.
	They're the one that that caused him or brought, brought it about, that caused him to do it at the last moment, that had you not been there, something would have been different or whatever . . . and that's why you have the tremendous guilt feelings.	It seems that I do have this feeling of responsibility—
	I know you do.	And I know I was puttin' pressure on him

Riley	Monroe
p. 12	But . . . you were the person he was closest to . . . and if he was gonna do it with somebody there, who else would he have done it with?	I've thought about it (unintelligible)
	. . . I don't think you actually saw the gun go off, I mean—	I couldn't have—
p. 12	I think you were lying on that sofa and . . . the noise obviously is what you remember as the sudden jolt or whatever.	I've had that to come, to come back to me so many times
pp. 12, 13	. . . Then your routine mechanism takes over . . . where you remember you need gas or you need to go to the grocery store . . . and little trivial things take over your consciousness.	That'd help me shut it out then.
	It helps you shut it out.	
p. 13	And then you wanna hope for the best. What did I see? I'm trying to believe I didn't really see it.	Yeah, I know that morning I was trying this all out. It can't be true. It can't be true.
p. 15	You know now what happened. You just have been overtired. You'll remember more details later. . .	I thought so much about. I like your, your (unintelligible) opinion about this and your insights, what you thought of it, and I don't know if I'll get to that point or not
	. . . it'll just take time.	
p. 20	And see, you suppressed all this until we got on that . . . got through that test yesterday.	. . . but I would feel it at least. I don't understand what was happening.
p. 23	I have all my questions answered as far as I'm concerned.	What about (unintelligible)
	I think we're pretty well on the same wavelength. . . . I don't see anything else that would have . . . brought it up. There's only two alternatives, and I took, the other one I just don't contemplate.	

Despite these efforts by Riley to restate a position that Monroe never held, Monroe remains politely firm. She does not adopt Riley's premise although she does accept Riley's hypothetical that routine mechanisms take over one's consciousness in such circumstances, compliantly replying, "That'd help me shut it out then." That Monroe considered this a hypothetical is revealed by her use of the conditional "would," here found in a contracted form, "that'd." Not content with a hypothetical, Riley converts the verb to the present tense when he responds, "It helps you shut it out."

Riley then recycles his first-person tactic, "What did I see? I'm trying to believe I didn't really see it." Monroe's response is not particularly helpful to Riley's thesis although she admits she had considered it (". . . that morning I was trying this all out").

Finally, in a burst of confidence totally unjustified by anything found in what Monroe has said so far, Riley concludes, "I have all my questions answered," and, "I think we're pretty well on the same wavelength." The fact that Monroe gives no response is indicative either of the fact that they were, indeed, on *different* wavelengths or that Monroe believes that Riley finally believes her. A suspect who has not adopted the suggestions made by the detective in the preceding substantive topics could take Riley's statement to mean that he had believed her story, that Burde was not dead when she left, that she was telling the truth, that she did not see the gun in her lover's hand, that she left Burde's house when she said she did, and that she was not there when it happened. But this is not what Riley meant by his statements. On the basis of no language offered by Monroe, Riley interpreted everything to mean that she was agreeing with him, as the following diagram illustrates:

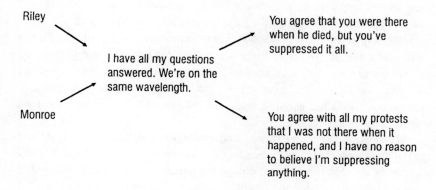

Riley

Monroe

I have all my questions answered. We're on the same wavelength.

You agree that you were there when he died, but you've suppressed it all.

You agree with all my protests that I was not there when it happened, and I have no reason to believe I'm suppressing anything.

It is not unusual for two people to understand two quite different things from the same statement. Clues to their different understandings are determinable from the overall context of what has been said up to that point. In this case, as the preceding topic-response analysis shows, Riley seems to believe that he was successful in his efforts to convince Monroe that she left Burde dead, that she wasn't telling the truth, that she saw the gun with Burde's body, that she left the house later than she claimed, and that she was there when the death occurred. Monroe, in contrast, shows through her responses that she does not adopt any of Riley's hypotheses. Beginning with these two totally different perspectives on what had been said between them to that point, Riley's vague utterances about having all his "questions answered" and about their being "on the same wavelength" were bound to be understood quite differently. People interpret vague or ambiguous utterances on the basis of their knowledge of the world and infer meaning on that basis.

An important question must be considered here: Is Riley so absorbed in his own interpretation of what might have happened that he is not able even to hear Monroe's disagreements and non-adoptions? Some people are like that, of course, but such are ill-suited for the role of fact finder in a law case. Or was Riley so intent on netting Monroe as the murderer that he was consciously willing to overlook her lack of agreement, talk over and interrupt her responses while producing a tape recording that might not seem to support his own theory? Later listeners, such as prosecutors and even jurors, might grasp at ambiguities and turn them against Monroe. In addition, the factor of audio quality must be considered. Riley's voice is generally clear and loud. Monroe's is not. Would jurors remember what is loud, clear, and dominant better than words that are muffled, soft, and sometimes inaudible? Of course they would, explaining, perhaps, why the prosecution never produced a transcript that would equalize the jury's memory of the utterances.

It is neither appropriate nor possible to determine exactly which of these motivations caused Detective Riley to conduct this interrogation the way he did. If he was so absorbed in his own theory that he didn't listen to Monroe, he is not a very good interrogator. If he consciously overlooked, interrupted, or drowned out what Monroe said, the integrity of the process must be questioned.

Whatever Riley's motivation, his results were successful. Despite my testimony represented by the preceding discussion, the jury convicted Beverly Monroe of murder. Her coerced-compliant stance was apparently interpreted as an internalized admission of guilt, supporting Kassin's (1995) fear that the dangers of coerced-compliant and coerced-internalized confessions are the most difficult for law enforcement and court officials to comprehend. But Monroe's case was even worse. Although she was counseled, even hypnotized, into compliance, her actual words do not support a confession. Her compliance never reached admission of what she was accused of, and it is likely that the jury was contaminated by what they heard Riley saying, rather than by Monroe's own language.

Inferred
Confession

Most law enforcement agencies try to obtain confessions on video- or audiotape, on stenographic record, and in writing, or any combination of these forms. Indeed, virtually all confession cases I have analyzed have produced one or more of these confession records.

► Case Study of Shiv Panini

In one case I worked on, however, no tape, no stenographic record, no written confession, and not even any notes of the alleged confession were available at trial. The entire prosecution rested on the memories and interpretations of what two detectives and the suspect's supervisor at work claimed they had heard: a confession. Not surprisingly, the defendant claimed he did not confess to the act for which he was charged. The evidence in this case, then, rested on memories and perceptions of actual language, rather than on written or spoken records of that language.

The setting was a government research center (all names and places have been changed for confidentiality). The participants were Dr. Shiv Panini, a neuroimmunology researcher originally from Bombay, India; Dr. Paul Pavlick, his lab chief; Detective Harvey Chase of the agency police force; Captain Joel Brown, also with the agency police; and Dr. Itoko Omoto, an agency researcher who brought the suit against Dr. Panini.

Dr. Omoto, the junior member of the group, originally was under the mentorship of Dr. Panini. From deposition testimony, it became clear that all was not well between the two and that by spring of 1992, Dr. Omoto believed that Dr. Panini was trying to block his progress at the institute. His belief was that Dr. Panini was unhappy that Omoto had gone behind his back directly to their lab chief, Dr. Pavlick, for various favors and that he was moving up the career ladder too quickly.

Toward the end of March, Dr. Omoto suddenly began to observe cell deaths in his lab experiments. Suspecting Dr. Panini, he called in the agency police to investigate the matter. Detective Harvey Chase responded, and he and Dr. Omoto devised a plan to capture the person whom they believed to be guilty of tampering with Dr. Omoto's experiments.

Detective Chase's first idea was to rig up a video camera in the lab to run during off-hours, when they believed the tamperer damaged the cells. Three times they tried this, and three times the camera failed. But did it? During his deposition, lab chief Pavlick mentioned that he had reviewed the videotape. When questioned about this, Detective Chase admitted that he had taped over one tape on which Dr. Panini had been seen. When asked why he did this, Chase explained that nothing unusual had been noted on this tape and that it was, therefore, of no value to the investigation.

Detective Chase and Dr. Omoto also devised a scheme for getting fingerprints on the containers of Dr. Omoto's experiments. They were successful in this effort—so much so, in fact, that they got the fingerprints of most of the researchers in the lab. As it turns out, the target containers were kept in a refrigerator in the lab and were accessible to all who used it. Several experiments were conducted simultaneously, and it was common practice for the researchers to move containers around in the refrigerator. To be sure, Dr. Panini's fingerprints were on the containers, but so were the prints of others.

Finally, a card-key time check of the lab revealed that Dr. Panini had used his card to enter the lab after-hours at the time when one of the tamperings was alleged to have taken place. It is not unusual for scientists to check on their research in off-hours, and the fact that his card did not show entry on other alleged tampering dates did not support the allegation that he was the culprit.

The inconclusive evidence of the videotape, the fingerprints, and the card-key entry times did not deter Detective Chase, who decided to confront his only suspect, Dr. Panini, with the accusation. The way this confrontation took place formed the only evidence in the case.

As outlined in his deposition, Detective Chase had been trained in the *Reid technique* of interviewing and interrogation. The focal point of the training is the Reid Interview Tabulation Sheet, a 4-page form containing a warning of rights (with waiver signature) on one page, a medical data sheet on one page, and two pages containing 15 numbered questions the interrogator should ask. To the right of the questions is a small space in which the interrogator writes down the suspect's responses to these questions, along with three boxes marked T, D, and ?. *T* stands for truthful; *D* stands for deceitful; and *?* stands for uncertainty about truthfulness. The Reid technique calls for the interrogator to ask each designated question, record each answer, and judge each answer's veracity.

Detective Chase dutifully attempted to carry out the method in which he was trained when he interrogated Dr. Panini. The exact circumstances of how this interview came about are a bit murky because the various participants present somewhat different versions. The following appears to be at least close to accurate.

Once Detective Chase decided to confront Dr. Panini, he telephoned Panini's office. Dr. Panini was not there at the time, and the secretary took a message to call Chase back (no association was made with the agency police). When Dr. Panini called his office and was given this message, he asked to speak to Dr. Pavlick, his lab chief, to see what it was about. Dr. Pavlick refused to tell him what it was about but urged him to make the call to Chase. Panini did so and made an appointment to see Chase the next day at Chase's "office." On arriving at Chase's office, it became apparent to Dr. Panini that he was at the agency police office. He entered anyway and reports that he was immediately asked to sign a waiver of his rights. Refusing to do this without seeing his lab chief first, Dr. Panini then went to ask Dr. Pavlick about this matter. Panini's report of that meeting was that Pavlick again refused to tell him what it was about but directed him to go back to Chase.

On returning to Chase's office, Panini was once again asked to sign a waiver of rights, which he again refused to do unless he was told what the whole affair was about. It should be noted that this procedure violates the accepted practice of gathering information (interviewing) before reading the subject his or her rights and subsequently interrogating. Both men then went to another room, and Detective Chase began asking the questions on the Reid Interview Tabulation Sheet, beginning with the medical data page. On completion of this information, Dr. Panini reports that Chase told him, "Dr. Panini, I know you did it." Panini's response was, "I want to see my lab chief." Then Chase asked either the Reid interview question (Chase's testimony) or, as Panini reports, "What do you do when anybody has a problem in cell culture?" Panini reports that he told Chase the things that are done and that he had, in fact, been giving Dr. Omoto advice on this issue. Chase then asked what that advice was, and Panini answered "media check, fetal bovine serum, sodium, nonessential amino acids, glutamine, and 2ME." To this (again according to Panini), Chase asked, "What is the name of that reagent again?" To this, Panini replied, "2ME, why?" Chase then asked Panini to write it on a piece of paper because "that's how the issue of this reagent came about."

At this point, Chase left the room and returned with another man, unknown to Panini but later revealed to be Captain Brown, whom Chase had asked in to be a witness. Again they asked Panini to spell the reagent, which he did. Panini then reports that Brown said, "We know you did it. . . . we have you on videotape, we have your fingerprint, and we have your record of entry." Panini reports that he denied doing anything and once again asked to see his lab chief.

Panini went directly to Dr. Pavlick's office, where, Panini reports, his lab chief told him, "I spoke to the deputy director yesterday, and he agreed with me that you have to be terminated right away." Panini asked, "Why?" To this, Pavlick replied, "Shiv, I know you did it. . . . get a lawyer and go see the tape." Panini again pled his innocence and then left.

Detective Chase's deposition offers a somewhat different view of his meeting with Dr. Panini. Chase reports that Panini was "ashamed and embarrassed" when he arrived, offering a weak denial, "I didn't do it," with no follow-up, no raised voice, and as Chase put it, "no body language. . . . He said it just to say it."

Chase's training in the Reid technique had prepared him to use "themes, to find some common ground as to why the person did what they did." Chase reports that he hit on the following theme:

> Dr. Omoto's very aggressive nature as far as him wanting to move ahead faster and faster, and I used a theme that you were just trying to teach him a lesson, weren't you, to slow him down, he was moving too fast and that's your job, you're his mentor, if you think he's going too fast, he's going to make mistakes, and he's going to mess an experiment up, so that's why you did this, didn't you, you were trying to slow him down. And that's where I got a connection . . . that Itoko (Omoto) had gone over his head to Pavlick and gotten permission to do experiments, and that was confounded by the fact that Omoto didn't keep him informed of his progress in his experiments, basically he just left Dr. Panini out in the cold and wasn't keeping him informed at all.

Chase reports that Dr. Panini agreed with this, shaking his head, while "I just kept expounding."

When questioned further, Chase admits that this "theme" was his own creation and that Panini gave no verbal response, no verbal agreement: "He was really upset. He was mad."

Both Panini and Chase agree that at some point in the meeting Chase left the room. Panini said they both came back into the room together, but Chase tells it differently: "I don't know what he (Brown) witnessed . . . actually I wasn't standing right in the room with them, I was standing around to the side." Chase does point out, however, that Brown told him that Dr. Panini "admitted to using the 2-Mercaptoethanol (2ME) and that he said that this was the first time that he'd ever done that, tampering with somebody's experiment."

The rest of Chase's deposition dealt with the Reid Interview Tabulation Sheet and how Chase filled it in. Not all the questions on the sheet were asked of Panini, including Question 14, which asks about alibi. Ten of the 15 questions call for the suspect's opinions or speculations. Question 14, the unasked one, calls for the suspect to report facts. Curiously, Dr. Panini, in his deposition, states that he does not recall being asked any of these 14 questions.

When I was called by Attorney David Wilcox to consult with him on this case, I was dismayed by the lack of evidence I had to work with. Usually, there is at least a written confession, and it is not uncommon to have audio- or videotaped interrogations as well. Here we had only the memories and perceptions of Chase, Brown, and Pavlick to compare with the memory and perception of Panini. We began in the hole, quantitatively, three witnesses against one.

First, I examined the depositions of Panini, Chase, Brown, and Pavlick to ascertain consistencies and inconsistencies of their memories and perceptions of what happened during the conversations in which the confession allegedly occurred. Needless to say, I found many differences. Panini reported considerably more of the conversation than any of his accusers. The most interesting difference, however, was in how Chase and Panini report the lab's problems with the cell cultures, noted above. Having introduced the theme of jealousy as motivation for Panini to commit tampering, Chase inferred that when Panini nonverbally agreed (with head shaking), he was agreeing that he, indeed, tampered. Panini, in contrast, reports that he agreed to giving Dr. Omoto advice on his problem and that, after he mentioned 2ME, he was accused of "doing it." Curiously, neither Chase's nor Panini's deposition testimony specifies a confession having occurred.

These two reports also reveal an important similarity: Both Chase and Panini use the pronoun *it* to refer to a preceding event or situation. Chase reports what he calls "weak denials" when Panini responded to his accusation, saying, "I didn't do it." In contrast, Panini repeatedly reports that he asked why he was there, what this was about, and that he wanted to see his lab chief. To the second accusation, this time by Brown, "We know you did it," Panini reports that he asked, "Did what?"

The pronoun *it* is crucial here. The specific accusation of tampering with the experiment was not reported in the depositions. All references are to *it*. If *it* had been defined clearly and unambiguously as tampering, Panini might have denied this even more strongly. The question is, What did Panini think *it* referred to at this point in the conversation? He apparently agreed that Omoto had reason to be unhappy with him. He admits to giving Omoto advice about what to do about cell death in his research. But no antecedent for *it* is made explicit beyond this.

The deposition of Dr. Pavlick also sheds some light on his conversations with Dr. Panini. First, Pavlick reports that Panini began the meeting by apologizing. Panini does not mention this. It is the nature of Indian culture to be embarrassed and apologetic when called before a superior in a tense situation. Such behavior would seem marked to an outsider to this culture but would be considered normal, accepted behavior by an insider. Second, Pavlick also reports that Panini acknowledged that he would have to leave the agency "under those conditions." The meaning of "those conditions" was not reported or specified in Pavlick's deposition and were left to Panini to infer. Any number of inferences, including bickering between researchers, were available to Panini. Even though Pavlick reports that Panini "acknowledged" this, Panini's report differs greatly. Panini says that his response was, "Why?"

This difference in memory and perception between Pavlick and Panini is significant because Pavlick had reported earlier in his deposition that he couldn't remember what tense Panini used and what pronouns Panini used when he allegedly said that Omoto and another researcher "were or are" plotting against him. Pavlick's imperfect memory of the verb tenses and pronouns suggest strongly that such imperfection might well apply to other pronouns in the same conversation. Pavlick reports, for example, that Panini said, "I did it to teach him, or them, a lesson."

Usually, when analyzing a deposition, the linguist has only the written version to go on. But at one point during Panini's deposition, the court reporter was asked to read back a question. In the transcript, the court reporter explained that this deposition was not being produced stenographically but, instead, was being tape-recorded. Noting this, I asked the attorney to try to secure a copy of the tape recording. He did so, and I was able to determine that Dr. Panini is very soft-spoken, which often made it difficult for even the prosecutor to hear what he was saying to her. Pronouns are often the most difficult words to make out in recorded conversation. "We did it" and "He did it" sound amazingly similar sometimes, and even "I," "we," and "you" are often confused.

Because there was neither a tape recording nor a stenographic written representation of the original interrogation of Panini, because Panini's voice is quiet, and because Pavlick admits to having difficulty determining the pronouns and tense markers Panini used, there is considerable reason to believe that Pavlick's report is less than accurate.

Chase, Brown, and Pavlick all claim that Panini confessed to tampering with Dr. Omoto's cell culture, causing cell death, yet their deposition testimony leaves gaping holes in exactly how, or if, such a confession happened. First, Chase claimed that Panini confessed during his administration of the Reid interview. Then, Brown claimed that Panini confessed to him, either with or without Chase being present, depending on whose report is accurate. Finally, Pavlick claimed that Panini confessed to him although we have nothing more to go on than his word for it, soundly denied by Panini.

A closer look at the Reid technique may enlighten things a bit because the confession motif began at that point:

Interview	T	D	?
1. Do you know why I have asked to talk to you here today?	___	___	___
2. We are investigating the (issue). Did you (issue)?	___	___	___
3. Who do you think (issue)? Now, let me say this if you only have a suspicion I want you to tell me that, even though you may be wrong. I will keep it confidential and not report it to that person. Who do you think (issue)?	___	___	___
3a. Is there any reason that you can think of that someone would name you as a suspect?	___	___	___
4. Is there anyone you know well enough that you feel is above suspicion and would not do something like (issue)?	___	___	___
5. How do you feel about being interviewed concerning (issue)?	___	___	___
6. Do you think that (issue)?	___	___	___
6a. Why do you think that victim is saying you are the one who did this?	___	___	___

Interview	T	D	?
7. Who do you think would have had the best chance to (issue)?	___	___	___
8. Why do you think someone (issue)?	___	___	___
9. Did you ever think about (issue) even though you didn't go through with it?	___	___	___
10. Tell me why you wouldn't do something like this.	___	___	___
11. What do you think should happen to a person who would (issue)? (Why?)	___	___	___
12. How do you think the results of the investigation will come out on you?	___	___	___
13. Do you think that person who did this would deserve a second chance under any circumstances? (Why?)	___	___	___
14. Alibi — Details	___	___	___
15. Is there any reason why . . . . Now I'm not saying that you did this but . . .	___	___	___

NOTE: T = Truthful; D = Deceitful; ? = Don't know.

The first question to ask of this interrogation procedure is whether it follows the guidelines of an effective interview. Reid is coauthor of the book *Criminal Interrogation and Confessions* (Inbau et al., 1986), in which law enforcement officers are advised to tape-record confessions and interrogations. If tape recording is not possible, they should be stenographically reported. If Chase had followed the advice of the author of the Reid technique, considerable light would have been shed on an otherwise confusing situation. If Panini had, indeed, confessed on tape, the matter would have been over quickly and efficiently.

The point of an interrogation is to find facts that are subsequently submitted to intelligence analysis and, finally, submitted to the advocacy of prosecution. The Reid technique appears to require the interrogating officer to be fact finder, analyst, and prosecutor. Ten of the 14 questions asked call for speculation, opinion, or perception, not for facts. Even then, one of the few fact questions, 14, was unexplainably omitted.

Interrogation manuals uniformly suggest that questioning is most effective if the suspect is first asked an open-ended question that enables him or her to tell his or her story uninterrupted. At that point, the officer can follow up with *wh-* questions for the specifics of who, what, where, and when. Then, probes follow, usually with questions that can be answered with either a yes or a no. The principle here is that the best evidence is that which is self-generated and not influenced by the question or the questioner. This pattern is not followed by the Reid technique. Half of the questions are yes-no type, interspersed throughout, rather than flowing from, broad (open-ended) to narrower (*wh-*) to yes-no probes.

Perhaps most damaging of all is the fact that the Reid technique does not take into account cultural, social, or individual differences in question answering. It apparently ignores the fact that most Asians, Southeast Asians, Africans, and many Latins consider it a challenge and very impolite to maintain eye contact. Indians, in particular, avoid body contact publicly, even hand shaking, and they consider eye contact to be equal to body contact. Chase marked lack of eye contact as deceptive on the tabulation sheet on several occasions, possibly because the Reid manual says that suspects should have eye contact 30% to 60% of the time if they are truthful.

The Reid technique also makes much of body language as an index of truth or deception. Chase mentioned body language as one "key" that he relied on to form his interpretations. Nervousness, body twitching, and arm movements are considered a "key" of deceitfulness despite the fact that instruments such as the Psychological Stress Evaluator (PSE), Mark II Voice Analyzer (PSA), the Hagoth, and the Voice Stress Monitor all detect *only* stress, not lying (Ekman, 1985, p. 98). Ekman comments further, "there is no sign of lying per se, only negative emotions. The manufacturers of these rather expensive gadgets have not been too forthright in cautioning the user about missing liars who feel no negative emotions and misjudging innocent people who are upset" (p. 98).

Ekman's own extensive research on nonverbal cues to lying focuses on facial expressions, particularly the forehead and the mouth, noting with sophisticated machinery and multiple replayings (not on-the-spot judgments) that a synchrony of these movements is required for genuine emotions. Of eye-blinking, for example, he notes that it can be involuntary, but increases involuntarily when a person is emotionally aroused, and is common when a person is fearful of being misjudged.

Body movements and cultural differences, as was noted earlier, are overlooked by the Reid technique. When Indians are accused of something, they evidence extreme nervousness, body twitching, and downward glances. They are ashamed of being so ill-thought-of and become quiet, passive, and helplessly humble.

The Reid technique also apparently overlooks important social differences. For example, it fails to take into consideration the fact that certain professionals, such as academics, elaborate broadly on topics with which they are familiar. Chase placed great emphasis on the fact that Panini gave unnecessarily detailed responses about the problems of cell death, but this detail could be expected of a research scientist talking about his field of expertise. Chase interpreted Panini's excessive details as deceptive and marked the D box to the right of the question despite the fact that Ekman (1985) observes that "the lie catcher is vulnerable to errors unless he knows what the suspect's *usual* emotional behavior is like" (p. 96). In any case, contrary to the advice of the Reid manual, giving detailed answers is considered the sign of truthfulness (Porter & Yuille, 1996).

Evidence of Panini's academically oriented elaborations can be found more than 30 times in his deposition, even to simple yes-no questions. His style is to elaborate on topics with which he is familiar, not unlike other academics, as any lawyer who has cross-examined experts comes to appreciate. Like other academics, Panini also requests clarification some 40 times in his deposition in an effort to be clear about what the prosecutor is asking. This, too, is a language characteristic of the academic researcher and one that can be quite frustrating to the questioner, who, like Chase, could easily interpret such behavior as digressive or off-topic.

The Reid technique also fails to consider individual differences in that it does not call for baseline knowledge of a suspect's verbal and nonverbal behavior in order to use this as a comparison with behavior elicited in an actual interrogation. Even the much-maligned polygraph tries to establish baseline behaviors before any interpretations of deception are made.

Finally, the Reid technique asks the interrogator to do more than is humanely possible: to elicit facts and opinions, but also to determine, on the spot, whether the suspect's answers are deceptive. Not only is this task overload, but it is virtually impossible to make a better than chance determination of deceptive behavior in that way. In their recent review of the research on deceptive communication, Miller and Stiff (1993) conclude, "these findings lead us to conclude that humans are poor lie detectors. . . . In general, people are only slightly more accurate than a coin flip when making judgments of truth and deception" (p. 69). One of the greatest problems in the attempt to determine truth from deception, according to Miller and Stiff, is "the misplaced confidence people have in their detection skills" (p. 70). Given a principle to follow, detectives like Chase will rely on it as though it were a proven fact. Chase, unfortunately, was a victim of the Reid technique, which led him to believe that by observing nervous behavior, eye avoidance, excessive details, long pauses, and other so-called keys to deceptive behavior, he was actually observing deception. What he was not told was that such keys are highly variable by culture, by occupation, and by individual temperament and condition. Such variables can make the keys useless, even dangerous, methods of determining veracity. Nervous behavior may be an indication of deception, but it is also an indication of many other things. The situation of being interrogated can easily create nervousness, whether or not the suspect is lying.

Other than the work of Porter and Yuille (1996), research on deceptive behavior has been amazingly silent about verbal clues to deception. Most of the work has been carried out on nonverbal clues, with the inconclusive results noted above. One thing about verbal clues that has been established, however, is found in the language of the interrogator, not the suspect. If a question is asked in such a way that the interrogator displays skepticism, the suspect tends to increase eye-blinking, hand gesturing, and response length. Miller and Stiff (1993) report several studies over the past 15 years that "found when people receive feedback indicating that others are suspicious about the validity of their statements, they modify their behavior to become convincing" (p. 91).

Detective Chase also considered Panini's "lengthy" pauses an indication that he was being untruthful. Yet lengthy pauses are typical of Indians. To respond quickly is considered impolite. Because I was able to secure a tape recording of Panini's deposition, I was able to note that he regularly paused overly long, by American standards at least, before answering many of the prosecutor's questions. It is reasonable to believe, therefore, that he paused in much the same way when Chase interviewed him.

Other elements of Panini's language also shed light on Chase's interpretation of his veracity. Panini is a native speaker of Hindi who learned English as a second language. Almost universally, speakers of a second language "translate" the phonology, syntax, and discourse style from their native language into their new language. Some of these translations may seem minor, but others can mislead the native English-speaking listener into thinking the person is saying something different from his or her intentions. The following is a list of some of the translations Panini makes:

noun-verb reversals	I realize what is this place.
	What kind of problem you are having?
flexible syntax	I went in with him some room
	It all depending in the incubator where is the space.
	I'm not going to talk to you anything.

omission of definite articles	that's incubator
	it was not broad project
	only after seminar
collective nouns	I wrote a three grants
	and the Dr. Moul was also passing cell lines
omission of prepositions	looking effect of morphine
	these two things are looked
	what we are talking
omission of pronouns	no need to repair (them)
	I saw (you) on the tape
verb harmony problems	they are trying to accusing me
	he didn't just sat down
	so I have spoken to my chief before I talked to Sairi
deletion of subject and verb	then (you are) not losing your time
translation of Hindi politeness honorifics (refer to honored person in third person)	Dr. Pavlick say you have been terminated
	Dr. Pavlick just say . . .
translation of Hindi verb *keh,* meaning "say," "talk," "speak," "tell"	I am not going to talk to you anything

I noted earlier how pronouns and verb tenses played an important role in Dr. Pavlick's recollection and perception of what Dr. Panini said to him. These samples of quotations from Panini's deposition illustrate not only his use of pronouns and verb tenses but also many other potential hindrances to a listener's perception of what he was saying.

Chase wrote very little about what Panini answered to his Reid interview questions. His attention apparently was on determining truthfulness or deceit. Much of what Chase recorded in the answer section were his own comments on Panini's answers, such as "very detailed," "afraid and fearful," "no eye contact," "weak denial," "guarded," "too many keys," "body language," and "weak answer." The crucial thing is that Chase did not record one word that might indicate that Panini confessed to tampering.

The government at first considered bringing criminal charges against Dr. Panini but then changed and brought a civil suit against him for damages incurred by the cell culture deaths. The trial took place in June 1994. By the time I was contacted, Dr. Panini's attorney, David Wilcox, had already submitted a witness list. Because my name was not on the list, we both realized that my major role in the case would be to provide information and analysis to be used in arguments and cross-examination. I might be used as a rebuttal witness if it became appropriate and useful to do so, but only if the judge agreed. It was a bench trial, and as it turned out, the judge wisely expressed his disapproval of the Reid technique early on, eliminating the need to present much of what I had to say. Nevertheless, Attorney Wilcox tried to get my testimony admitted on the last day of trial. The judge would not admit it. After the closing arguments, the judge asked for various briefs and took the case under advisement until later that month, when he found Dr. Panini guilty of tampering, as charged.

Unvalidated Confession

So far, we have discussed interrogations and confessions that had videotaped, audiotaped or, some semblance of notes or other records available for trial. The issue is verifiability. If the interrogators wish to validate that their procedures of interrogating were fair and that they followed accepted guidelines, then some sort of record must be produced. Such available record keeping includes

- ► Videotape
- ► Audiotape
- ► Stenographic record
- ► Detailed notes

The most useful method of validating and preserving a record is the videotape because it offers the most information. Videotaping, if done properly and effectively, displays nonverbal as well as verbal information. People can say words and sentences that convey one meaning, but when the same speech is captured on videotape, the nonverbal communication can suggest a somewhat different interpretation.

An audiotaped interrogation/confession preserves some of the features of a videotape, but it lacks essential nonverbal information and sometimes is less clear than videotape as to who is speaking at any given time, or to whom the person is speaking, or how far the speakers are from each other.

If a court stenographer records the interrogation/confession, still more information is lost, especially important intonation of voice that gives clues to the speaker's emotions, emphases, and hesitancy. Without at least an audiotape recording, pause lengths are unknown, and even long breaks in the interrogation may appear never to have occurred.

Note taking is the least informative method of preserving an accurate record of what occurred in an interrogation because there is no way of telling how accurate notes really are or what has been left out of them. But even notes are better than nothing at all.

► Why Did Kevin Rogers Confess?

Most cases discussed in this book had tapes (audio or video) of the interrogation/confession, a stenographically produced transcript of the event, or minimally, notes made by the police interrogators. But the case of *Texas vs. Kevin Rogers,* in June 1995, had none of these methods of verifying exactly what happened in the interrogation. Here, the Houston police produced only a confession, handwritten by the interrogating officer and signed by suspect Kevin Rogers. This document was produced after 7 hours of interrogation about the murder of Lilly Lockhart, a near neighbor of the 15-year-old Kevin. Amazingly, the police not only did not videotape or audiotape the interrogation (despite the fact that such equipment was available in the very room in which Kevin was questioned) but also did not make use of a police stenographer. They also claimed at trial that no notes were taken of this important event.

It is noteworthy that the Houston police habitually videotape interrogations of suspected burglars but choose not to videotape interrogations in homicide cases (Geller, 1992).

For the linguist who works with language data, this case had little to work with. When Houston attorney Obii Aham-Neze called on me to assist him with his case, I expressed my doubts about what I might be able to do because there was no linguistic data to analyze. Nevertheless, Aham-Neze sent me all the law enforcement reports on which the indictment was based. In the Michael Carter case (Chapter 5), the Baton Rouge police had audiotaped parts of the interrogation and then turned the tape recorder off after Michael started vomiting. Later, a written confession was produced and the interrogating office swore under oath that all he did was write down exactly, word for word, what Michael had said. In the case of Kevin Rogers, however, the police provided even less material for validation of the accuracy of what happened: no tape, no stenographic transcript, and no police notes—only the written and signed confession.

To understand the context of this alleged confession, some background is useful. On Saturday, May 5, 1994, at about 9 p.m., someone savagely stabbed Lilly Lockhart to death and raped her in her Houston home, leaving her naked body in a pool of blood. At the time of her attack, she had been talking on the telephone with one of her lady friends for some 45 minutes. When her friend heard Ms. Lilly call out, "Leave me alone," and then scream, the friend called 911 for emergency help. A squad car in the area responded within 5 minutes and found her already dead. Ms. Lilly's friend also called Lilly's brother, who lives in Houston, and told him to go quickly to Lilly's house to check on her. He arrived some 30 minutes after the police got there.

Not wishing to disturb any possible fingerprint evidence on the telephone at the victim's house, the responding police officer went to a neighbor's house, the Johnsons, to call his superior at the police department. The next day, Shelton Johnson, who easily overheard what the officer told his station about the murder scene, described these overheard details to his friends at school. Among those who listened to what Shelton reported from the police officer's call from his home telephone was Kevin Rogers.

Immediately, the Houston police deduced that the crime was the work of amateurs, so they began fingerprinting "all" the boys in the neighborhood (but, curiously, not Shelton Johnson) to compare these with the fingerprints found in Ms. Lilly's house. Officer Douglas, in sworn testimony, indicated that the police profile pointed to a youth offender, rather than to an adult professional killer. Among those local boys fingerprinted was Kevin Rogers, who agreed to give his fingerprints when the police assured him that they were fingerprinting "everybody." It was not long until the police found a match of fingerprints in the house with those of Kevin Rogers, making him a prime suspect. When the police questioned Kevin, they learned that he spent a lot of time at Lilly Lockhart's home, doing odd jobs such as cleaning her house. This information did not dissuade the police from believing that the reason they found his fingerprints was that Kevin was the murderer.

Another bit of necessary background information is that Kevin Rogers, though in eighth grade, functions as a second or third grader academically. His teachers testified to this, along with the fact that the Houston schools were committed to the practice of "social promotion," that Kevin's reading ability is at 2.8 grade level, and that he was in various remedial classes. The vice principal of his school testified at trial that he had never had a disciplinary problem with Kevin. The magistrate who was asked to witness that Kevin had knowingly signed the confession statement reported that the boy was neatly dressed, cooperative, well mannered, and appeared to be the product of a good family. A student Kevin was not. A nice kid Kevin was.

Armed with Kevin's fingerprints all over Ms. Lilly's house, the police thought they had their killer. One detective, in fact, noted in a television interview that Kevin was a "serial" killer. His interrogation took place with no warning. The police went to his school the day after the body was found, waited until the last class period, and then whisked Kevin to the police station for his interrogation. Once there, Kevin was read his *Miranda* rights and was asked whether he understood them. He said that he did even though the standard *Miranda* form contains such words as "right to remain silent," "right to have an attorney present," and "anything you say will be held against you in a court of law." Several times during his 7-hour interrogation, Kevin was again asked whether he understood his rights. On each occasion, he said that he did. Nevertheless, when Kevin finally was permitted to meet with his mother and, even later, with an attorney, he emphatically denied that he was the killer. These denials contrast with his signed confession, which is as follows, in all capital letters (numbers are added to each statement here to make referencing easier):

JUVENILE CONFESSION
Taken at 8300 Mykawa Rd., May 6, 1994.

1. I DO NOT WANT TO CONSULT WITH A LAWYER BEFORE I MAKE THIS STATEMENT, AND I DO NOT WANT TO REMAIN SILENT, AND I NOW FREELY AND VOLUNTARILY WAIVE MY RIGHT TO A LAWYER AND TO REMAIN SILENT AND I KNOWINGLY MAKE THE FOLLOWING VOLUNTARY STATEMENT.

2. I LIVE AT 3220 BINZ AND THAT'S ABOUT FIVE OR SIX HOUSES FROM MS. LOCKHART'S HOUSE.

3. I HAVE KNOWN MS. LOCKHART FOR ABOUT 2 YEARS.

4. SOMETIME I CALL HER MS. LILLIE.

5. MY MOTHER HAS KNOWN HER FOR A LONG TIME.

6. MY MOM KNEW MS. LOCKHART'S MOM.

7. MS. LOCKHART DIDN'T HARDLY LIKE ME BUT SHE WOULD LET ME COME TO HER HOUSE AND PLAY WITH HER LITTLE DOG, BERTRUM.

8. I THINK IT WAS LAST YEAR WHEN I WAS SHOOTING BIRDS IN THE TREES IN THE BACK YARD BEHIND MS. LOCKHART'S YARD AT NALOW'S HOUSE WAS WHEN SHE TOOK MY PELLET GUN FROM ME.

9. I BEEN ASKING MS. LOCKHART TO GIVE ME BACK MY PELLET GUN.

10. MS. LOCKHART ALWAYS SAID NO.

11. MONDAY, THE DAY THAT MS. LOCKHART GOT KILLED, I WENT TO SCHOOL.

12. WHEN I GOT OUT OF SCHOOL, I WENT HOME AND CLEANED UP MY HOUSE.

13. AFTER I CLEANED UP THE HOUSE, I WENT TO MS. LOCK-HART'S HOUSE.

14. I WENT INSIDE THE BACK PORCH AND PLAYED WITH THE PUPPY.

15. THE PUPPY RAN INSIDE THE HOUSE, AND I RAN INSIDE THE HOUSE BEHIND THE PUPPY.

16. THE PUPPY RAN UPSTAIRS, AND I RAN UPSTAIRS BEHIND THE PUPPY.

17. I HEARD THE TV ON IN MS. LOCKHART'S BEDROOM.

18. I LOOKED IN THE BEDROOM JUST TO SEE WHAT IT LOOKED LIKE.

19. THE PUPPY RAN IN THE OTHER ROOM WITH THE TWO BEDS.

20. THE ROOM IS TO THE RIGHT AT THE TOP OF THE STAIRS, THEN I WENT INTO THE BACK ROOM.

21. I OPENED THE WINDOW ABOUT (KEVIN RAISED HIS HANDS ABOUT 18 INCHES, SHOWING ME HOW HIGH HE OPENED THE WINDOW). I WAS GOING TO COME BACK TO GET MY PELLET GUN.

22. THEN I PICKED UP THE DOG AND I WENT BACK DOWN THE STAIRS.

23. MS. LOCKHART WAS IN THE KITCHEN, SHE GAVE ME A GLASS OF KOOL-AID, BUT I DON'T REMEMBER WHAT KIND OF KOOL-AID IT WAS.

24. I DRINK THE KOOL-AID.

25. AS I WAS LEAVING THROUGH THE BACK DOOR, I SAW THE KNIFE THAT I USED TO STAB MS. LOCKHART WITH LAYING ON THE TABLE IN THE LIVING ROOM BY THE DOOR.

26. THEN I WENT TO MY FRIEND JOHN'S HOUSE DOWN THE STREET.

27. WHEN I LEFT JOHN'S HOUSE, I WENT TO TEXAS SOUTHERN UNIVERSITY AND I PLAYED BASKETBALL.

28. THEN I CAME BACK TO MS. LOCKHART'S HOUSE.

29. I WALKED TO THE SIDE OF HER HOUSE, AND I SAW THE DOG PLAYING IN THE BACK PORCH.

30. I OPENED THE SCREEN DOOR, AND I WENT INSIDE THE PORCH.
31. THE DOG WENT INSIDE THE HOUSE.
32. I CRAWLED INTO THE LIVING ROOM WHERE MS. LOCKHART WAS SITTING ON A CHAIR TALKING ON THE PHONE WITH HER BACK TO THE DOOR.
33. I THINK SHE HAD ON SOME BLUE SILK PANTS.
34. I SAW THE KNIFE STILL LAYING ON THE TABLE IN THE LIVING ROOM, AND I PICKED UP THE KNIFE AND SHE HEARD ME AND TURNED AROUND.
35. SHE SAID SOMETHING.
36. I FORGOT WHAT SHE SAID.
37. I PUSHED HER TO THE FLOOR.
38. I TOOK THE KNIFE AND STABBED HER ABOUT THREE TIMES I THINK.
39. I STABBED HER IN THE CHEST.
40. I STABBED HER IN THE NECK.
41. I SAW HER BLOUSE OPENED BECAUSE IT CAME WHEN SHE WAS FIGHTING WITH ME.
42. I PULLED HER PANTS OFF OF HER.
43. I LAID ON TOP OF HER JUST FOR A FEW MINUTES, BUT I DIDN'T PUT MY PENIS IN HER.
44. I HAD MY PANTS OPENED WITH MY PENIS OUT, BUT I DIDN'T PUT IT IN HER.
45. I GOT UP AND LEFT THE KNIFE IN HER CHEST.
46. I SEEN SOME MONEY ON THE TABLE, AND THEN I TOOK THE MONEY UP.
47. I SAW MY PELLET GUN LAYING ON THE FLOOR BY THE COUCH. I FORGOT TO PICK UP THE PELLET GUN.
48. I WENT OUT THE SAME WAY I CAME IN THROUGH THE BACK DOOR.
49. I RAN HOME.
50. I AM SORRY FOR WHAT I DID.
51. I WISH THAT IT DIDN'T HAPPEN.

The perplexing issue is why Kevin would have signed the confession if he so emphatically denied that he did it. Could it be that school had taught Kevin to be cooperative and to not rock the boat? Schools engender cooperation based on trust. If the teacher says something, it is, by definition, true. The interrogation is, for a child like Kevin, an extension of the school. If the police officer said it, it must be true, whether or not Kevin understood it or agreed with it. In the mind of a cooperative child, a police officer, like Kevin's teachers, would not be likely to trick or trap him.

The evidence used to indict Kevin included three major elements: (a) his suspicious fingerprints, (b) his alleged apology (Statements 50 and 51), and more seriously, (c) this signed confession. To Attorney Aham-Neze, the fingerprints could be easily dismissed. The signed confession, however, was a much more difficult mountain to climb. Meanwhile, Kevin was indicted as an adult even though at the time of the murder he was only 15 years old. To make matters even worse for Kevin, he was charged with first-degree murder and faced a sentence of life imprisonment.

When the attorney called me, I was reminded of the Michael Carter case, and I suggested that he tape-record a sample of Kevin's speech. I wanted to determine whether such a sample might provide evidence that his language patterns and thought processes were consonant with what he had signed. Unlike the Michael Carter case, however, the police officer who wrote the confession statement that Kevin signed eventually declared that it was *not* a verbatim record of Kevin's own words. He described the confession process as follows: The interrogator sat at a word processor, asking Kevin questions. As Kevin answered, the police officer typed up the confession, not in Kevin's own words, but in approximations thereof. This process is similar to one formerly used (and much disputed) in Australia, called *verballing*.

Sources of Kevin's Knowledge

During his tape-recorded conversation with his attorney, Kevin recounted what he did on the day of the murder and on the following day, when he was interrogated and arrested. Although the tape could not be used to show that the confession language was not Kevin's, it did reveal some useful things. The more I listened to the tape, the more I came to realize that a major issue would center on the sources of Kevin's knowledge. The confession statement provided facts that could have had their source in three types of knowledge: (a) specific event knowledge (facts that only the killer would know), (b) general world knowledge (which anyone might know), and (c) secondhand knowledge (which anyone might be able to learn from someone else). For example, in his confession, Kevin states that he played with Ms. Lilly's dog (14-16, 22, 29-31), that Ms. Lilly was on the telephone (32), that he saw a knife on a table (25, 34), and that she gave him a drink of Kool-Aid (23-24). These are world knowledge sources for Kevin because he had visited her house regularly, played with her dog, saw her on the telephone, observed the things in her house as he cleaned it, and got refreshment from her. Secondhand knowledge is derived from other sources, as the following illustrate:

1. What Shelton Johnson told him and others when he overheard the police officer use the telephone in his home to report in to his station. This would include the fact that her blouse was opened (41), that she was stabbed in the neck and chest (39-40, 45), that money was taken (46), and that her underpants were off to the side of her (42).
2. What was reported over the television about the case, which included the fact that Ms. Lilly was on the telephone when she was attacked (32).
3. What the police told Kevin, directly and indirectly, when they interrogated him the following day, including the fact that Ms. Lilly was raped (43-44), that she was wearing blue (33, although Kevin notes that her pants were blue silk, whereas she was actually wearing a blue blouse), and that her underpants were off on the side of her body (42).

These facts were all interpreted by the police to mean that Kevin had specific (therefore incriminating) knowledge of the murder event, whereas each fact also had the potential of a more benign interpretation, and some, such as her blue clothing, were inaccurate. Without a verifiable basis, such as a tape recording of what the police actually asked Kevin during his 7-hour interrogation, we have no way of knowing exactly what Kevin was referring to when he reported these facts. We do not know the source of his knowledge. For that matter, because the confession statement contains only Kevin's alleged answers to the police officer's questions, we have no way of knowing whether he actually ever made these statements, or whether the interrogator's questions influenced or distorted Kevin's words, or whether Kevin's alleged answers were given in the sequence represented by the interrogator's report of the confession.

The major alleged incriminating facts in Kevin's confession statement are the ones in which Kevin is reported to have admitted to killing Ms. Lilly (37-45). Even in his taped discussion with Attorney Aham-Neze, Kevin admits that he signed this statement and that he knew, in doing so, that he was admitting his guilt.

Tape Recording Made by His Attorney

The tape recording made by Kevin's attorney months after Kevin was arrested and jailed serves as a model of how Kevin answers questions, how he thinks and responds, and what he believed, because the attorney's questions are clearly recorded along with Kevin's answers. Immediately apparent from this recorded conversation is that Kevin often does not understand even the simplest questions asked of him, as the following passages make clear:

Q: She (the magistrate) told you all that? (about your rights)
A: Yeah.
Q: Did you tell her you understood all of that?
A: Yeah.
Q: Did you really understand all that she was telling you?
A: No.
Q: Then why did you say you understood it?
A: I don't know.
Q: Have you ever been involved in anything where your rights were read to you before?
A: Yes.
Q: What situation was that?
A: I don't know.
Q: I mean, have you ever been involved in anything where somebody read you your rights, saying you have the right to remain silent . . . before that time?
A: No.
Q: That was the first time anybody's read you any of these rights?
A: Yeah.
Q: Did you understand what they were saying?
A: No, I was just listening to them. I know the right to remain silence, and I ain't say nothing and I ain't understand the others. I ain't know what they was talking about then, I knew the right to remain silent.
Q: How come you didn't request an attorney?
A: I ain't know.

Here we see two instances in which Kevin gives answers he subsequently contradicts: (a) that he understood his rights and (b) that he has been asked his rights on other occasions. He admits to understanding his right to remain silent but gives no evidence of understanding his right to have an attorney. His greater goal, made clear throughout his conversation and repeated in his testimony at trial, was to see his mother. He reports that he asked for her five or six times:

> **A:** I ask him there, and I ask him is my mama going to be at the juvenile to pick me up. They say she might, going to be there to pick me up.
>
> **Q:** OK, but did you ask for your mama before you gave the confession?
>
> **A:** Uh-huh. That's when I asked can I call my mama, before I done this confession.
>
> **Q:** What did he say then?
>
> **A:** No, wait until we go to juvenile.
>
> **Q:** And what did you do when he said, "No, wait"?
>
> **A:** I start crying, and they start asking me question. And that's when, you know, then I made confession.
>
> **Q:** What made you give the confession?
>
> **A:** They say I might be able to go home.

The issue of Kevin's request to have his mother with him prompted considerable debate. At trial, police witnesses denied that Kevin ever asked for her and maintained that they were following standard procedure at all times in this matter. Kevin may not have known what a right to have an attorney present meant, but he most certainly knew what it meant to have his mother with him. Perhaps he even thought this would be enough.

Finding a Possible Motive

When asked about the point at which the interrogation moved to the stage of typing up a confession, Kevin maintained that he denied killing Ms. Lilly, but certain answers triggered a change in the interrogation:

> **A:** I said I ain't do it, that I knew her for a long time, and I told him that I help clean up, cut her yard, and I go play with the puppy sometime. Then, then he asked me how did we get along. Then that's when I told him about the BB gun. That's when he left out, then he start talking to the other police

officers, then he had came back in, then he had took me to a room next door where a computer was.

Apparently, Kevin's mention of the BB gun introduced the motive the police were looking for. They drew out from Kevin that Ms. Lilly had once caught him shooting birds and had taken his gun away from him. She had kept it since. It was not difficult for the police to hypothesize than Kevin, in anger, had returned to her house to get the gun and, being rejected, turned on her and killed her. This theory, however, had a flaw: The BB gun was not taken by whoever killed Ms. Lilly (see confession statement 47):

A: They asked me why I ain't take the BB gun.

Q: And?

A: First, they said, well, you went in after a BB gun. I said no. I said I ain't want it because I already had, I already had a BB, a pellet gun. Then they say we got the BB gun, that's when they found my fingerprints on the BB gun too. They said your fingerprints on there. I said yeah. Then they say how you know your fingerprints on there? 'Cause, I said, it was mine until Ms. Lockhart took it from me.

Interesting here is the distinction Kevin makes between a BB gun and a pellet gun. Ms. Lilly had confiscated his BB gun, and he says he replaced it with a pellet gun. The confession statement 47 says:

I SAW MY PELLET GUN LAYING ON THE FLOOR BY THE COUCH. I FORGOT TO PICK UP THE PELLET GUN.

Despite the similarity of BB guns and pellet guns, Kevin chose to distinguish them here. The police did not. In any case, it is clear that Kevin's mention of his problem with Ms. Lilly over the BB gun creates the motive the police were looking for.

It is curious, however, that Kevin's continuous denial of killing Ms. Lilly did not trigger moving the interrogation to the confession statement stage, whereas the discovery of a possible motive did. If Kevin's recitation of the sequence of events is accurate, this means that the typing up of the confession statement occurred before there was a confession. Police testimony about this sequence neither supported nor contradicted Kevin's report.

Moving to the Confession Stage

At one point, the three police officers asked Kevin which one of them he would like to speak with alone. Because one of them was cursing him and calling him a liar, Kevin selected one who had been relatively quiet and calm. (At trial, the police all denied cursing at Kevin.) They then moved to another room, one that had a computer and printer, and the police officer began to type on it. Probing this unusual circumstance, Kevin's attorney asked Kevin:

Q: Wait a minute, what did you tell him, what made him leave to go talk to the other people, then take you to another room?

A: When I kept saying I ain't do it and I was telling the stuff that's true.

Q: What stuff did you tell him that's true?

A: That I ain't did that, that I knew her for a long time. And I told him that I help clean up, cut her yard, and I go play with the puppy sometime. Then he ask me how did we get along. Then that's when I told him about the BB gun. Then that's when he left out, then he start talking to the other police officers. Then he had came back in, then he took me to a room next door where the computer was.

It appears that once the possible motive was deduced, Kevin's reported world knowledge and secondhand knowledge were promoted, in the interrogator's mind at least, to specific event knowledge. This process is not uncommon in everyday conversation, but it has no place in an expectedly rigorous police interrogation, in which any inferential leaps must be well grounded and validated. In just such matters, in fact, video- or audiotape validation would remove any doubts about interpretation or procedure.

Promoting Secondhand Knowledge to Specific Event Knowledge

If Kevin's account to his attorney is accurate, we can gain some insights into how his secondhand knowledge was promoted to specific event knowledge. Immediately following the above passage, Kevin continues:

A: Then he said, Do you know anybody else that can do something like that? I said no. Then I start telling about Shelton, how he came to school talking about what happened. . . . I told them Shelton came to school talking about how she *got killed. She got her throat cut and got stabbed in the heart and then she got raped.*

Noteworthy is the fact that when Kevin reports the facts of Ms. Lilly's death above, he uses the passive voice. We will come back to this later. The taped interview continues:

Q: Was he typing at this time, when you were telling him that?

A: Uh-huh. . . . He say they had my fingerprints around the house, like inside. And that's when I told them that I go over there and help clean up.

Q: So he was typing something, and you had not yet agreed to give a confession at that time?

A: Uh-huh . . .

Q: You never agreed to give him a confession?

A: No . . .

Q: But you didn't say to him, I'll give him a confession?

A: I ain't know what that was.

Q: You didn't know what what was?

A: The confession . . .

Q: Because he said that you, after about 30 minutes you told him that you had agreed to give him a confession.

A: I ain't say confession.

Q: You told him that you did it?

A: Uh-huh, 'cause that's when he start hollering at me and stuff. He said if I hurry up my mama might be at the juvenile waiting for me. . . . Then I just said I done it. I thought I was going home.

To this point, it is clear that Kevin indeed admitted to killing Ms. Lilly, but serious questions could be asked about why he admitted it. In his own words, he did so to see his mama and get out of a situation in which he was being hollered at and told that he was lying. It is also noteworthy that Kevin did not even know what a confession was; this supports early arguments that his mental development was far below what might be expected of a 15-year-old. The interview with Kevin's attorney continues:

Q: Tell me what happened when you entered the second room.

A: I told him about Shelton.

Q: What question did he ask you that brought up Shelton's name?

A: He said, how you know about all of this . . . what happened to Miss Lockhart. I told him I saw it on the news this morning. Then when I got to school, this boy told me about what happened. . . . I said that *her neck got cut and got stabbed* 'cause I was telling him what I heard Shelton say.

Q: When did you tell him that?

A: When we was in the second room and he was typing it up. . . . He say you know what happened to her, huh? I said, yeah. Then he asked me, what? I say she *had got killed,* somebody stabbed her . . .

Q: Pick it up from there.

A: And I said, he came to school talking about how *she got killed,* and start telling everybody around school.

Q: Go on, keep talking.

A: Then he say, that mean you didn't really do it. I said, no. Then he said, why did you say you done it? I say, I'm ready to go home. I want to go home. . . . He say, you ain't going to be able to go home until we finish. . . . And I start telling him the stuff Shelton said. . . . I say I ain't killed her. Then I just said that she got, that *she got cut in the throat, then got stabbed.* Then that some money came up missing. Then they said, you know something about her blouse being open. I said no.

Q: Did you know what color blouse she was wearing?

A: Huh-uh. They said she had a blue blouse on. I said, I ain't know, 'cause I ain't know what happened. . . . Then he ask me did I rape her. I said no, I ain't do it.

Q: The color of the blouse, how did you know that?

A: 'Cause he said something about the color.

Q: Who said that?

A: The officer that talking to me. . . . They said her blouse was open. I say I don't know. I said Shelton said something about *she got raped.* Then he didn't say nothing. Then he said how you know? I said he had told me about, that money came up missing.

Q: Shelton told you that?

A: Yeah. He the one told everybody about it . . .

Q: OK, what else?

A: They said money came up missing, and they said, how much money you took? I said I ain't take no money.

I noted earlier that when Kevin describes the killing as he knows about it, he does so using the passive voice. In the italicized passages above, we see further instances of this. This practice contrasts with other statements that Kevin makes, in which he uses the active voice (e.g., "I ain't do it," "I said," "I went," "I play with"). An educated, cunning liar may well be able to do the same thing, but Kevin is in no way educated, cunning, or clever. It would take considerably more linguistic and mental capacity than Kevin has to pull off such language skill. In addition, reporting events in the passive voice is consistent with secondhand knowledge, not firsthand experience. This passage also reveals Kevin's secondhand knowledge about the blouse being open (police told him this), about Ms. Lilly being stabbed in the neck (Shelton told him this), about money being taken (Shelton told him this), that she was raped (Shelton told him this), and about the color of her blouse (the police told him this). The reporting of information that is learned from secondary sources is not evidence of original, firsthand knowledge unless the reporter is cunning and clever, which Kevin is not.

The Knife

Another fact about which much was made in this case concerned the knife that was used to kill Ms. Lilly. The confession statement mentions the knife on four occasions:

25. AS I WAS LEAVING THROUGH THE BACK DOOR, I SAW THE KNIFE THAT I USED TO STAB MS. LOCKHART WITH LAYING ON THE TABLE IN THE LIVING ROOM BY THE DOOR.
34. I SAW THE KNIFE STILL LAYING ON THE TABLE IN THE LIVING ROOM, AND I PICKED UP THE KNIFE AND SHE HEARD ME AND TURNED AROUND.
38. I TOOK THE KNIFE AND STABBED HER ABOUT THREE TIMES I THINK.
45. I GOT UP AND LEFT THE KNIFE IN HER CHEST

In the tape-recorded interview with his attorney, Kevin discusses the knife as follows:

Q: OK, well tell me, so you know what kind of knife she had?

A: No.

Q: . . . The statement that you seen the knife laying on the floor and you picked it up. How did that statement come into it?

A: I just said I saw a knife.

Q: You just said you saw a knife. Tell me what you told the officers about the knife.

A: I just told them that I saw a knife on, like on a table like.

Q: When did you see that knife?

A: Like, um, when I had walked through the kitchen going in the—

Q: Remember, but that you're saying that you deny that you killed her. How come you told them that you saw the knife and you grabbed the knife and she was on the phone?

A: I say I ain't grab the knife.

Q: But in the confession you said you grabbed the knife and you walked toward her and she turned around. Tell me, why did you tell the officers about that?

A: I just said it.

Q: What did you tell the officers about the knife?

A: I said I grabbed it.

Q: You'd been denying it all this time. What made you decide to say that you grabbed the knife and walk toward her?

A: 'Cause they say I had to use a knife 'cause what they found in her chest.

Q: And then when they say you had to use a knife, what did you say?

A: Then that's when I said I grabbed the knife.

Q: Go on.

A: Then they say, "You stab?" Then I said, "No." Then they said, "Why you grab a knife?" Then he start cursing and said, "You lying." Then I said, "Yeah."

Q: Tell me . . . about the knife again.

A: They said that I had to use a knife. Then they say—

Q: How did the conversation come up that you had to use a knife?

A: 'Cause they say, 'cause I had, that's when I told them there was a knife on the table.

Q: How did you tell them there was a knife on the table if you weren't there?

A: That was, Shelton just, I was just listening to what Shelton was talking about.

Q: When you talked about the knife, were you still reporting what Shelton told you?

A: Uh-huh. . . . I was telling them about what Shelton told me, then they said that she got killed with a knife. Then I just told them that I saw a knife on the table, then they said that.

Q: So they told you that she got killed with a knife?

A: Uh-huh.

Q: And then you said you saw a knife on the table?

A: Uh-huh.

Q: Why did you say you saw a knife on the table if you weren't there, if you were still telling them what Shelton told you?

A: I don't know. I was just saying, 'cause I was ready to go home. . . .

Q: What made you admit that you grabbed the knife, because you were still saying what Shelton said. How did it go from Shelton said to "I grabbed the knife?" Tell me that.

A: They said you had to use a knife.

Q: And you said what?

A: And then I said, I just grabbed it.

Q: When they say that you had to use a knife, why didn't you say that you didn't kill her?

A: I say I ain't do it.

Q: Well, how did it come to the point where you told them what Shelton told you, then you talked about grabbing a knife? What made you jump from what Shelton was telling you to you doing it?

A: 'Cause I ain't know what happened until Shelton told me.

Q: OK, so when the officers were telling you, how did you switch from what Shelton was telling you to you doing it?

A: 'Cause that when they said I had to use a knife.

Q: Ok, then what did you say?

A: That I had grabbed it. Then I had said she just got stabbed. She got stabbed. But I didn't say I stabbed her. I say she got stabbed.

Q: When they told you that you had to have done it with a knife, what did you say?

A: Then I said I grabbed the knife.

Q: Then what did you do when you grabbed the knife?

A: Then I say she got stabbed.

Q: Then did you say where she was stabbed?

A: In the chest and throat.

Q: How did you know where she got stabbed?

A: From when Shelton told me.

Q: Who else told you where she was stabbed?

A: It was on TV once. It say a stabbing of Ms. Lockhart.

Once again, we see a secondhand fact, one that Kevin derived from Shelton, being promoted to firsthand, experiential evidence. The knife topic was introduced by Shelton and then reported by Kevin to the police when they told him he had to have used a knife. Most people would not be convinced by such logic, but Kevin is not most people, so he tells the police that he grabbed it, hoping, perhaps, that this would satisfy them and be the end of it. Through a convoluted logic that only Kevin could concoct, he believes, though he admits to grabbing the knife, that he avoids inculpating himself by using the passive voice about what happened to Ms. Lilly, saying: "She just got stabbed. But I didn't say I stabbed her. I say she got stabbed."

Kevin maintains, even after signing his confession statement, even after admitting that he grabbed the knife but didn't stab Ms. Lilly with it, that he has preserved a record of his innocence. From his perspective, he signed the confession, knowing that it was not accurate, knowing that he did not kill Ms. Lilly, only so that he could see his mama and go home. He admitted to grabbing the knife even though he steadfastly maintains that he was not even at Ms. Lilly's house and could not have done so, only because he felt trapped in a logic that he did not comprehend.

The Apology

The confession statement includes two items (50 and 51) that were considered an apology by the prosecution:

50. I AM SORRY FOR WHAT I DID.
51. I WISH THAT IT DIDN'T HAPPEN.

These so-called apologies were considered very important during trial, allegedly offering proof that Kevin did what he was accused of.

In the tape-recorded interview with his attorney, the following exchange took place regarding this apology:

Q: Did you tell them you were sorry that it happened?
A: Uh-huh.
Q: You said you were sorry that it happened?
A: Uh-huh.
Q: That you shouldn't have done it?
A: No, I ain't say that.
Q: What did you say?
A: I said I'm sorry for what happened. Then they say, did you stab? Then I said no. Then they said, why you grab a knife? Then he said, start cursing and said, you lying. Then I said, yeah. Then, then that's when he said, you sorry for what happened? I said yes.
Q: When did you say you were sorry?
A: Like after when they ask me, are you sorry for what happened? I say yes.

Three times during this interview, Kevin reports sorrow over what happened to Ms. Lilly. Nowhere does he apologize for having committed the crime or, as Statement 50 of his confession reports, "for what I did." In any case, the speech act of apologizing has three characteristics:

1. It must be for an offense committed by the apologizer or group that the apologizer represents.
2. It must be specific as to the event for which the apology is made.
3. It usually includes a promise of no future offenses.

An apology differs from a condolence in that the latter:

1. Is for an offense that is not caused by the person offering the condolence.
2. Need not be specific as to the event for which the condolence is made.
3. Includes no promise of future offense to the person offended or hurt.

Even if Kevin's words, "I am sorry for what I did," were accurately reported, such words are not specific as to the event for which the alleged apology was made, and they offer no promise to abstain from future offenses. The vagueness of these words suggests that, even if accurately reported, they could refer to any number of things, including Kevin's previous offense with his BB gun. Because we have no context in the typed confession statement, we have no way of knowing, even if Kevin said this, to what it refers. In any case, the confession statement as a whole gives conclusive evidence that Kevin's sources of knowledge were conveniently overlooked, if not distorted. Ability to be insensitive to such sources of knowledge suggests strongly that other reports of his interrogation could be treated in an equally cavalier manner.

The second "apology" statement, "I wish that it didn't happen," can in no way be construed as an apology. If accurately reported, it better fits the speech act of condolence than the speech act of apology. Like condolences, it is nonspecific and consistent with an event not caused by the person offering the condolence.

At trial, Attorney Aham-Neze went through the 51 statements in the confession with Kevin, one at a time, asking him whether or not he said each one. Kevin said yes to 12 (24%) and no to 39 (76%). The only ones Kevin agreed that he said were 2, 3, 4, 5, 6, 8, 9, 10, 11, 12, 27, and 51, those having to do with where he lived, how well he and his mother knew Ms. Lilly, the BB gun incident, that he was in school and then played basketball the day of the murder, and that he said, "I wish that it didn't happen." He agreed with many of the statements in a general sense—for example, that he often played with her puppy and that he was at her house regularly—but he did not agree that he did these things on the day in question. He agreed he knew the things that Shelton told him, that he heard on the television news, and that the police told him, but he did not agree that his knowledge of these things came about as a result of any personal, experiential knowledge. It is possible to imagine that the interrogator could misunderstand Kevin because he is far from articulate. But the fact that Kevin showed, in his tape-recorded conversation with his attorney, that he can articulate such matters clearly and unambiguously makes one wonder why a trained police investigator could not have figured this out too.

Conclusion

The expression "shooting fish in a barrel" seems to be an apt metaphor for this case. It would seem that the more questions one might have about a person's guilt, the more safeguards one might take to validate and accurately represent what happened during the interrogation. Apparently, the Houston Police Department does not subscribe to this principle. This leaves us with the belief that the department is willing to take full advantage of children, those whose mental capacities are below normal, and possibly others as well.

The judge in Kevin's trial would not permit me to testify at a hearing to suppress the confession statement. Nevertheless, Attorney Ahem-Neze asked me to come to trial and be prepared to give testimony there. As might be expected, the judge again refused to admit my testimony although he willingly granted that I was an expert and that my field of study was academically recognized and acceptable. After he refused to let me testify, I left my work product, including charts, with the attorney, who did his best to represent it, but Kevin Rogers was convicted of first-degree murder and is now serving a life sentence in prison.

Perhaps linguists should not even try to address cases that lack a videotape, audiotape, stenographic record, or notes of the event. We usually work with data, not the absence of them. Perhaps my trying to piece together the possible sources of knowledge by comparing it with the tape-recorded conversation between Kevin and his attorney goes beyond the limits of what a linguist can legitimately do. Even today, I am not sure about this. But I thought it was important to give it a shot, and I leave this record of what I tried to do for others to accept, or reject, or, I hope, improve.

An Effective Interrogation and a Valid Confession

10

So far, this book has catalogued flawed police interrogations and confession events, but it would be grossly unfair to law enforcement on the whole to give the impression that the cases cited here are representative of general practice. This is far from the case. Indeed, effective and conscientious police interrogations result in valid confessions. Indeed, in many instances, the suspect's *Miranda* rights are presented fairly. Not all interrogations misperceive the spoken words of the suspects or twist them, consciously or unconsciously, to achieve the appearance of guilt. Many law enforcement agencies make a clear record, often on tape, of the entire interrogation and confession. Only a few interrogators confuse their role as fact finders with the role of intelligence analysts as theory builders and interpreters. Even fewer interrogators try to play the role of psychologist or therapist, hypnotically planting suggestions in the minds of suspects. The cases described thus far are aberrations from the norm.

To present a contrast with the confession cases described thus far, it would be useful to see how two effective and conscientious District of Columbia law enforcement officers conducted their interviews that led to a valid confession. Toward this end, the case of *United States v. Pamela Gardner* (pseudonym) serves as such a model.

▶ Case Study of Pamela Gardner

In April 1992, the Washington, D.C., police found the mutilated body of Gerald Seeley within their district. Later, some distance away, they also discovered the badly beaten body of Hilda Barton, apparently dumped in the bushes near the Washington Arboretum. Barton would eventually recover and testify that her assailant was Donald Wharton, the male partner of Gardner.

Wharton had a murky past. He convinced Gardner that he was a security officer by showing her his badge, handcuffs, and other law enforcement equipment. In the past, if not concurrently, he had posed as a real estate agent, breaking into lock boxes and committing various burglaries.

Gardner was separated from the father of her two children and had entered into an on-again, off-again relationship with Wharton, who frequented her D.C. apartment but also spent considerable time in Richmond, Virginia. Gardner's ex-boyfriend provided some support for the children produced by their relationship, but he did not like Gardner hanging around with Wharton. For this reason, Wharton disappeared from view anytime he was apt to be at Pam's apartment. Gardner also had a 6-year friendship with Gerald Seeley, a man in his 60s who lived with Hilda Barton; Barton resented any attention that Seeley might give Gardner and assumed, unfairly, that their relationship was a romantic one. For this reason, Barton forbid Gardner's calls or visits to Seeley's home, causing them to meet surreptitiously, often in an alley behind his house. To Gardner, Seeley was a father figure, however, who often helped her out financially and in other ways. Gardner, 34-years-old, had no police record and had never been in serious trouble before.

After Seeley's body was found and after Barton had been rushed to a hospital, the police discovered that Barton's credit cards were missing. Quick police work revealed that the cards had been used the following day at Landover Mall to the tune of some $4,500. From that same mall, Gardner telephoned home to check on her children and was told by her sister that the police were there and that she should get home quickly. Her sister wouldn't tell Gardner what it was all about. Gardner returned home, where Detective Corboy met her, took her to police headquarters, and interrogated her.

Three interrogations of Gardner took place in this case. One was on the evening of April 13, 1992, the day following the murder of Gerald Seeley. The second was the following morning, April 14, at 1:05 a.m. Both interviews were conducted by Detective William Corboy. The third was on July 29 of the same year, this one by Detective Daniel Whalen, also of the D.C. police.

The first thing to note about these three interrogations is that they were videotaped in their entirety. Detective Corboy explains to Gardner during the first interrogation the reason for taping:

Corboy: It's been recorded in this room, as everything in this room is . . . and it's recorded for one particular reason . . . so there won't be any misstatements as to what came out of your mouth. . . . It won't be my recollection and my notes and only my notes and my recollection. . . . It is exactly as we speak in this room. That is the reason this room is set up that way . . . and that is the reason why I wanted to be sure that we used this room . . . so that there'd be no misstatements . . . no misunderstanding about what I said to you and what you said in response to that.

Detective Corboy's insights here are significant. If tape recordings had been made of the interrogations of Shiv Panini, that dispute could have been resolved easily. Without such a tape, even an audiotape, it was the interrogator's perception and recollection versus Dr. Panini's perception and recollection.

Critics of tape-recorded interrogations argue that such practice only offers the defense inroads to attack the prosecution. This is true *only* if the interrogation is flawed with unclear questions, misperceptions of what was said by both parties, interruptions, impatience, and generally inept or inappropriate interviewing procedures. When the interrogation is *not* so flawed, tape recording offers no inroads at all to the defense, as the *Gardner* case eloquently demonstrates.

Question Types and Sequence:
Detectives Corboy and Whalen

As was noted in earlier chapters, open-ended questions are recommended if the questioner wishes not to influence the respondent's answer, no matter what the setting. If teachers, for example, want to find out what students know, the least effective way to do this is to ask tag questions, such as, "Tin is the leading export of Bolivia, isn't it?" The tag part of the question, "isn't it," explicitly tells the student that this is the correct answer, and no real information is learned about the student's knowledge. Even the yes-no question (one that can be answered with either a yes or a no) is a poor measure of what students know because students have a 50% chance of guessing the right answer. Questions that offer the listener a choice of possible answers, like multiple-choice questions, also limit the range of what students know because guesses can be made. The best way to find out what students know is with open-ended questions and with *wh-* questions (who, what, where, how, why).

These two types of questions are also most effective in police interrogation when the goal is to discover what a suspect really knows.

The sequence in which these question types are used is also important. Conventional wisdom of police interrogation is first to permit the suspects to tell their stories, uninterrupted, before any probing takes place. The theory is that suspects will generate their own guilt, set the table for inconsistencies, slip up in some way, and generally paint themselves into a corner. This is less true, of course, for accomplished liars or for those who have had the time and skill at constructing believable alternatives to their guilt. Nor does the theory cause innocent suspects to implicate themselves in the crime; this is one strength of the approach.

Once the open-ended questions have been asked and the suspects have told their stories, the interrogator would do well to ask *wh-* questions to fill in the incomplete information about when, who, where, and so on. To this point, the suspects' responses have been relatively uninfluenced by the inter-rogator's questions. Finally comes a point at which yes-no questions can be asked because the narrative has been basically established by the suspects and the *wh-* questions have been answered.

Good police interrogations generally follow this question sequence, the same way that effective classroom teachers do. A structural assessment of poor interrogations (assessments that examine question types and sequences, rather than the content of the answers) reveals that open-ended questions are either rare or nonexistent and that the questioner relies far too heavily on yes-no and even tag questions. Such reliance puts the interrogation in jeopardy of being attacked by a skillful defense attorney, and the prosecution may well lose the case for reasons that may have nothing to do with the guilt or innocence of the suspect.

A simple tabulation of the question types (except for requests for clarification) used by the detectives in the *Gardner* case displays their competence as questioners as follows:

	Interview	Open-Ended	Wh-	Yes-No	Multiple Choice	Tag
236 Q's 144 pages	1	10	143	80	2	1
120 Q's 73 pages	2	12	54	50	3	1
82 Q's 61 pages	3	7	36	38	1	0
	Totals	29	233	168	6	2

Of significance here are (a) that so many open-ended questions were asked that *wh-* questions outnumber the easier-to-ask yes-no questions and (b) that so few choice and tag questions were used. Equally important, however, is the sequence of question types employed by Detectives Corboy and Whalen. Consistent with their task of trying to determine the facts without influencing the suspect's answers, they generally adhered to the following strategy:

First: Ask open-ended questions
then: Ask *wh-* questions
If necessary: Probe with yes-no questions
then: Repeat the cycle with another open-ended question

After the open-ended question, they asked *wh-* questions to fill in the facts and then probed individual answers to *wh-* questions with appropriate yes-no questions. Once satisfied, they returned to another *wh-* question pattern and stayed with *wh-* questions until it seemed necessary to probe with a yes-no question. This pattern was apparent throughout the three interrogations as the detectives moved from broad (*wh-*) to narrow (yes-no) and then back to the next section of broad questions again.

The hallmark of such questioning strategy is focus, patience, and control. Detectives Corboy and Whalen are singularly blessed with these qualities, at least in this case. Such patience is crucial with this suspect because it became almost immediately clear that she was telling one lie after another.

The content of the suspect's answers, of course, also dictates the questioning strategies and sequencing. Gardner's inconsistent responses were soon recognized by Detective Corboy for what they were: lies. Much of the first interrogation, in fact, consists of his gentle reminders that she was lying (24 times) and warnings to her to tell the truth (29 times). Thus, Detective Corboy asked many yes-no questions during this interview (80 out of 236 questions).[1] Even in the second interview, hours later in the same day, Gardner returned (with her mother), presumably to set straight some of her inconsistencies and to explain why she gave such misstatements (her reasons were that she was intoxicated and that she was so afraid of her boyfriend that she lied to extricate herself from the whole affair). Detective Corboy was still skeptical of what she told him, however, and had to probe her answers with yes-no questions in 50 of his 120 questions. Even so, Detective Corboy's questioning strategy followed the open-ended to *wh-* to yes-no sequence. Once Gardner's answers became transparently inconsistent (about 30 minutes into the first interrogation), her content clearly required many yes-no questions as follow-ups to her less than complete and forthright responses to his open-ended and *wh-* questions. The common interviewing problem is not yes-no questions in themselves, but with asking yes-no questions *before* asking open-ended and *wh-* questions and with asking far too many yes-no questions, especially when the situation calls for *wh-* and open-ended questions.

The success of Detectives Corboy and Whalen in asking such a high ratio of open-ended questions in these three interviews is evident from the lengthy responses given by Gardner when such questions were asked. If the intent of the interrogation was to permit the suspect to self-generate her story, for whatever reason, these detectives were extremely effective.

The down side of using open-ended questions is that the interviewers do not have as much control of the event. Detectives Corboy and Whalen had to sit patiently through several long, disjointed, and sometimes inconsistent renditions by the suspect, to keep track of her wanderings, and to organize, on the spot, what follow-up questions to ask to set her responses into the orderly framework they needed.

The Conversational Style of Detectives Corboy and Whalen

The police interview is, by definition and practice, a somewhat ritualized question-answer speech event, much like some doctor-patient interviews and, unfortunately, like far too many school classrooms. Obviously, the interview differs greatly from much of daily communication between friends and family.

A major difference between the interview and everyday conversation stems from the inequality of status and power of the police interrogator and the suspect. For example, in everyday conversation, in which the participants are equals, both can ask questions, introduce topics, disagree, and give directives. But in a police interview, these communicative devices are permitted only to the more powerful and higher-status participant, the police officer. The suspect is in the role of subordinate.

This role differentiation causes certain things to happen in the interview. If the indisputable goal of the interview is to discover facts that were hitherto unknown or unverified, the interviewer faces the problem of overcoming this preexisting power asymmetry. For example, if the goal is to get the suspect to self-generate facts, the suspect must be given the opportunity to introduce topics. If the interviewer wants the suspect to understand the questions asked, the interviewer must allow the suspect to ask questions, not just answer them.

Although it is well known that the person who asks the questions exerts certain power over the person who is to answer them, the police officer must suspend such power to achieve the goal of conversational style in the interview.

Also in other ways the power asymmetry of the police interview can be defused by the detective, including the use of a conversational style that downplays the question-answer routine and makes the event seem more like a conversation. Everyday conversations take place in the informal or casual registers (or styles). In contrast, court proceedings and other, more formal events take place in the formal register. Many language features distinguish the informal register, including the use of contracted verb forms, feedback markers (e.g., *uh-huh, right, OK, I see*), varied intonation patterns (rather than a flat, more formal tone), and indirectness rather than directness.

Long stretches of the three interviews by Detectives Corboy and Whalen show no responses by them other than "uh-huh," "OK," and "I see." In everyday conversation, listeners give such feedback as an indication that they are indeed listening and that they will continue to let the other person speak without being interrupted. Such feedback is polite and cooperative in itself, but it also tells the suspect that this is a conversation, not a grilling.

Other politeness tactics also characterize the interviews by Detectives Corboy and Whalen. In the informal conversation, the listener tries to take the point of view of the speaker. Detective Corboy accomplishes this perspective with statements such as the following:

p. 67   "I know that you're afraid. And, who knows, when a person is afraid, they obviously make the wrong decisions."

p. 123   "What he does is he uses you."

p. 126   "Maybe he has threatened your children. Maybe he's threatened you."

These comments enable Gardner to have some dignity and save face. What is remarkable is that, by this point in the interview, it has become quite clear that Gardner's story is inconsistent and probably untruthful. Despite this, the detective is not excessively confrontational about her lies. To be sure, he has repeatedly warned her about her misstatements, as the following sample shows:

p. 39   "What's happening here is you're digging yourself in a hole. . . . This is an opportunity for you to get back on board, *OK?*"

p. 40	"Now listen to me for a second, OK? Because this has *sort of* gone on long enough, *OK*?"
p. 43	"It's going to get worse for you and your *family, all right*?"

Notice especially how the detective mitigates his warnings with tags such as "OK" and "all right." Notice also how he presents her inconsistencies in the context of her family and how he mitigates how long this lying has gone on with the qualifier "sort of." He could have called Gardner a bald-faced liar. He could have shouted and stormed. He could have been far more direct. Instead, Detective Corboy keeps his composure and sets his warnings to be truthful in a more conversational tone.

Another example of how the detectives took the perspective of the suspect is evident by the fact that Detectives Corboy and Whalen not only ask questions but also often explain why they are asking them, as the following examples illustrate:

I.	p. 13	"And the reason that I ask, I was surprised you said you were unemployed because when I spoke to your children today, I was at your house, spoke to your sister, they were of the impression, they told us that you had gone to work."
I.	p. 19	"The reason I ask is I thought earlier you said something about you had to go to the rental car place today. Was I mistaken?"
III.	p. 26	"What we're doing here, we keep jumping back and forth in time. . . . We'll try and reconstruct this the best way we can, OK?"

Persons in power do not need to explain why they are asking questions or how they plan to process the answers. When they do make such explanations, however, it tends to level the playing field, reduce the asymmetrical relationship of the participants, and therefore encourage elaboration.

Finally, the suspect's perspective is taken by Detectives Corboy and Whalen in a more subtle and inconspicuous way: They do not interrupt Gardner, and they allow significant silence to take place after she has finished talking. Their sensitivity to the potential damage that interruptions can cause is evident by their almost total lack of interrupting Gardner. The one point at which Detective Whalen thinks he may have interrupted her occasions his following apology:

III.	p. 22	"Now, during the day—were you done with that? I didn't want to cut you off."

As it turns out, Gardner did not feel interrupted, and no important volunteered information was apparently lost.

Allowing a brief period of silence after the speaker appears to have finished a thought has long been recognized as an effective interviewing technique. I have taught this strategy to my linguistic students for years. If the point of the interview is to get a great deal of the informant on tape and only a little of the interviewer on tape, silence is the interviewer's ally. This is because people, Americans in particular, abhor a silence and tend to fill it up whenever it occurs. A 3-second pause in a conversation seems deadly, and people tend to feel uncomfortable unless something is being said. Effective interviewers use this knowledge for their own purposes, refraining from jumping in with another question until it becomes obvious that the speakers have, indeed, said everything they intended to say. Detectives Corboy and Whalen are in no hurry. They permit such silences and are often rewarded by Gardner's elaboration. Such elaboration, in fact, signals Gardner's downfall. She adds what she believes to be convincing details, but the inconsistency of these very details causes the detectives to understand that she is being less than truthful.

Everyday conversation includes personal comments of various types. The formal register does not. Throughout their interviews with Gardner, Detectives Corboy and Whalen give every impression of being human and personal, a fact that contributes greatly to the conversational tone of the interviews. The following examples are illustrative:

p. 3	"*Can I ask you to do me a favor* and put your purse down on the floor there?"
p. 103	"So *in your heart your values are* that you want to try to tell the truth."
p. 120	"This guy David . . . you've had a relationship with him of some sort. Did you have intimate relations with him this past weekend when he was here? . . . *I don't mean to pry,* but I'm just asking."
	(Gardner responds: yes we do have that type of relationship)
	"I just wanted to, OK, that's, that's, we don't need to go into that any further."
p. 126	"Is there *some barrier between you and I* that prevents us from talking truthfully about what happened?"

In these examples, Detective Corboy makes personal requests, evaluates Gardner's values positively, apologizes for his very personal question, and asks her to assess what it is about him that might be causing her to be less than truthful. The powerful person in an interview does not need to apologize, request permission to ask a question, or expose his or her own skill or competence to analysis. But clearly, the detective has decided to try to reduce the power asymmetry here by speaking in this way. Once one adopts the conversational mode, one either goes all the way with it or is forced to switch from one persona to the other.[2] It may seem contradictory for a police officer to give up or reduce his or her power in the interview. Indeed, it *is* contradictory because there can be no question about the power asymmetry of suspects with an investigation officer. The fact that they are suspects in itself produces the asymmetry, regardless of their social standing, education, or wealth. But if the goal of the interview is to get the suspects to feel free to talk, to elaborate, to self-generate their own guilt (the best kind of evidence), the officer would do well at least to try to reduce that asymmetry by giving up some aspects of power. This is not to say that interviewers should humble themselves unduly, degrade their office, become supplicants, or any other such extremes. But it is possible to make the interview more like a conversation between equals, even though the legal setting would indicate otherwise, and give up some of the power tools that could otherwise be used. For example, the detective does not need to give the appearance of being all-knowing. The television detective Columbo made effective use of his appearance of simple ignorance, as did, in real life, Senator Sam Ervin of North Carolina, whose down-home questions during the Watergate Hearings gained him national prominence. It is difficult to dislike Columbo or Senator Ervin, largely because their self-effacing postures, such as Senator Ervin's "I'm just a country lawyer," endeared them even to their detractors.

Detectives Corboy and Whalen by no means overdid their efforts to reduce their power. It is always clear that they are law enforcement officers in charge of an investigation. But they also make no claim to omniscience, as the following examples indicate:

- ► "This is what confuses me, OK."
- ► "Can I ask you to do me a favor?"
- ► "I don't mean to pry but . . ."
- ► "Is there some barrier between you and I . . ."
- ► "I was surprised you said . . ."
- ► "I thought earlier you said . . . was I mistaken?"

▶ "I just don't think that we've gotten to the truth."

▶ "I'm sorry, Pamela, but I really don't even want to be in this position with you because it's important that you tell the truth."

The all-knowing, all-powerful interviewer would not admit to confusion, request a favor, apologize for prying, be surprised, be confused about what was said earlier, mitigate his belief that she was lying, and be sorry about being in the position of pushing her to tell the truth. By even admitting that a "barrier" may exist between them, Detective Corboy is not placing the blame for this barrier entirely on Gardner.

Detective Whalen, in the third interview of Gardner, continues the strategy of non-omniscience begun by Detective Corboy:

p. 4   "*I believe* that on that day you were in this office"
p. 4   "*I believe,* looking back on it, that he also advised you of your rights"

Detective Whalen could have been certain about these matters, rather than expressing them with mitigated certainty, but he chose not to do so. This humanized his office and, in a sense, helped level the playing field a bit.

It should be stressed here that the advantage of reducing the power asymmetry and leveling the playing field is conceived not only out of a concern for human rights and dignity. A much greater advantage to law enforcement is that, by taking a one-down position on the one hand, by leading from behind, suspects are more likely to generate their own guilt, whether by producing inconsistencies in their stories or by simply confessing their guilt. Taking a hard line, throwing around one's weight, outright accusation, and tough guy hostility, on the other hand, are more likely to be met in kind. Detectives Corboy and Whalen are superior interviewers who give every evidence of recognizing the need to use sensible question sequences in a conversational style and from a level playing field.

During her second interview, Gardner admitted to lying in her first session. But even then she still didn't reach total truth. Some 3 months later, in her third interview, she came a bit closer but was still not totally forthright. Not until the trial itself did all the facts become clear. Gardner was indeed with Wharton the night he killed Seeley and attacked Barton. She heard the gunshots (although she didn't witness the killing), rode with Wharton to dump Barton at the arboretum, spent the night with Wharton, and fraudulently used Barton's credit cards the following day.

In contrast with the role of law enforcement in the other case studies described in this book, the D.C. detectives offer a hopeful model. Not only did they ensure a clear and complete public record by videotaping their three sessions with Pamela Gardner, but they also gave every evidence of being highly competent public servants. They gave the suspect the opportunity to self-generate her own guilt. They let her introduce topics, rather than keeping tight control over the direction of the interview, especially at the beginning. They encouraged Gardner's self-generation by often remaining silent even after Gardner appeared to have finished what she was saying. It is ironic that sometimes the best thing to do is to do almost nothing at all. The detectives were in no apparent hurry, evidencing patience and politeness at all times. Even when they had ample opportunity to be critical, their responses were controlled and mitigated. Their question sequence went systematically from open-ended to *wh-* to yes-no questions, not vice versa. They seldom, if ever, interrupted Pam, even when she wandered from relevance (*relevance* is a relative term, and the wise officer will let the subject define his or her own issues of relevance, unimpeded by law enforcement's own interpretation of it). The interview was conversational, not rigidly Q and A. The register was casual, not formal. The detectives did not display their own knowledge or superiority and even assumed a self-deprecating tone. They provided feedback marker "uh-huh" responses throughout, showing interest in what Pam was saying even while they probably disbelieved her. They explained procedures clearly. They even apologized for one errant appearance of interrupting her. They had no need to resort to anything as simplistic or dangerous as the Reid instrument (see Chapter 8) to carry out their task effectively.

When it was over, the detectives had gotten most of the truth from Pamela Gardner, or at least enough of it to go to trial. During the trial, still further confessions were elicited, but the case was made by these two detectives. Wharton was sentenced to 47 years to life. For Pamela Gardner, the government recommended 5 to 15 years.

▶ Notes

1. The questions tabulated here exclude requests for clarification.
2. The epitome of such switching of personas is commonly found in police interrogations, often with two different officers, one taking on the good-guy role and the other the bad-guy.

Some Basic Principles of Interrogation, Confession, and Deceptive Language

11

W rightsman and Kassin (1993) report that confession evidence is relentlessly regular in the courts, with an estimate of 47% of cases in Los Angeles, 68% of cases in New York City, 50% of cases in London and Birmingham accompanied by confessions (p. 1). Wigmore (1970) notes that a confession is the most influential type of evidence, and McCormick (1972) observes that the confession makes all other aspects of a trial seem superfluous (p. 316). Despite this, confession evidence can have serious problems, as the cases in this book illustrate.

Most criminal cases I've worked on have had no confession. The subjects have either not waived their constitutional rights or not come even close to confessing what law enforcement alleges they did, and therefore the cases came to trial without police interrogations and, of course, without confessions. Cases in which the alleged confession has played an important role in the trial—in my experience, at least—constitute only a small percentage, somewhere around 5% of the total cases I have worked on. What is clear, however, is the problematic nature of the confessions that have been made available to me over the past 15 years. It is difficult to say whether issues of constitutional rights, truthfulness, interrogation strategies, or the accusations of a participant about the crime allegedly committed by someone else are most problematic. Each of these types of confession even has its own potential for blocking the wheels of justice.

When controversy arises over whether suspects have actually waived their rights, the intentions of law enforcement are not called into question. It is quite natural in everyday life, as in the interrogation event, for two people to misunderstand each other. Words such as "I wanna" and "I don't wanna" have a way of sounding quite similar, especially when uttered quickly under heavily emotional stress. Police interrogators are not perfect under such conditions, but nobody else is either. When a tape recording is made of the interrogation, however, and the controversy is resolvable, we still do not have solid evidence of the police officer's intent to misconstrue the situation. Nor do I make any such accusation here. Linguistic analysis can ferret out the language facts that have occurred, but it cannot ascribe intentions of the interrogators. Their interpretations of what happened can be justifiably challenged, but not their motives. The same can be said of every other case described in this book, including even the detective who played the role of amateur therapist in the Beverly Monroe case. Such techniques can be questioned, but there is no scientific way to judge motives. In retrospect, one can question the jury verdicts, as in the cases of Steve Allen, DeWayne Hill, and Beverly Monroe, but such questioning also goes beyond the scope of linguistic analysis.

Law enforcement has made errors in the past and will probably continue to do so. We are all fallible. But if anything stands out from most of the cases reported here it is that law enforcement should make it a practice to tape-record the entirety of all interrogations, including confession events. On the surface, such advice might seem to be a plea to aid the defense in pointing out inconsistent or sloppy procedures, ambiguous questions, and memory lapses of police officers, as in the cases of Steve Allen, DeWayne Hill, Chris Jerue, and Jessie Moffett. But such a procedure can aid law enforcement even more. If Detective Carey had tape-recorded his initial meetings with Jessie Moffett, for example, he might have avoided the inconsistencies found in his own reports. It is particularly important for interrogators to protect themselves from accusations of going beyond prescribed limits when they make use of the types of trickery that Inbau et al. (1986) describe as acceptable and legitimate police procedure. When one engages in trickery, one invites the suspicion, even accusation, that such trickery is deliberately trying to confuse the suspect, rather than to get at the truth.

In the alleged confession of Michael Carter, we hear part, but not all, of the interrogation event. After Carter began to sob and vomit, the tape was turned off before any confession could be heard. Presumably, Carter regained his composure and, if the police report is accurate, then recited a confession that was taken down "word for word" by the police. Why wasn't this recorded? If the detective was accurate that Carter actually had said the words exactly as they were written down, a tape recording would have settled the issue. By tape-recording Carter's nonconfessional crying and denials of guilt and by not tape-recording the "actual" confession, the police invite disagreement and challenge.

Virtually every tape case I've worked on during the past 15 years has involved a missing tape. Often, the first conversation, the one that allegedly establishes the predicate, the predisposition to commit a crime, is not taped. Occasionally, as in the Moffett and Allen cases, important tapes have been lost. In both instances, the government attempted (and, succeeded, amazingly enough) to submit a transcript that had been prepared before the tape was lost, despite the fact that only tapes, not their transcripts, are considered evidence in most criminal trials. To avoid the embarrassment of sloppiness or incompetence, it is important not only to tape-record but also to establish an orderly system of preserving and retrieving such tapes for trial.

The various cases described in this book point to five principles for which future police questioning of suspects might benefit:

► Be Conversational

Law enforcement agencies distinguish between interrogations and interviews. If one were given the choice between these, the alternative is obvious: the interview. This is because interrogations are more accusatory, their intentions being to elicit a confession. *Interviews* are fact-finding events, somewhat neutral efforts to find out what the interviewee knows, did, or believes. Neither interviews nor interrogations are like conversations, which are more open and free. In a conversation, both parties become equal, a fact that encourages self-revelation. Self-revelation is, indeed, what police interrogators desire. If suspects self-generate their own guilt, the interrogation is clearly successful. If the investigator has to paint the suspect into a corner, the task is much more difficult, and the opportunity for criticism becomes more evident. The more the interrogation looks like an interview, the less the opportunity for such criticism. Likewise, the more the interview looks like a conversation, the less trouble the law enforcement officer will have with defense attorneys.

At issue here, then, is how to make the interrogation become more like an interview and how to make the interview become more like a conversation. The first step in removing the onus of the interrogation (and, at the same time, reducing the resistance of the suspect) is to level the interactive playing field as much as possible. In most conversations, participants are equals in status and power. They are not as equal in an interview, where the interviewer has the power of asking all questions, giving all directives, and introducing all topics. They are even less equal in an interrogation, where, in addition to the above advantages, the interrogator has the power to accuse, disagree, warn, and complain.

Therefore, if the goal is to get the suspect to self-generate information, even guilt, it is useful to make the communication event as much like a conversation as possible, where equal power and status permit such self-generation. The question then becomes, How can the asymmetrical power relationship of a detective and a suspect be made less asymmetrical? One way is to adapt to the informal speech register of conversation, rather than to the more ritualized register of law enforcement. The use of contractions (e.g., *don't, she'll*), rather than full forms (e.g., *do not, she will*), personal comments (e.g., apologizing, thanking, offering concerns for health), frequent use of feedback markers (e.g., forms like *uh-huh* and *yeah*, uttered while the suspect is talking), varied intonation rather than monotone, and the use of indirectness rather than directness are some of these conversational strategies. It is always the case that, in the search for knowledge, truth, and justice, the powerful adjust to the powerless, teachers adjust to students, the wealthy adjust to the poor, and the native speaker adjusts to the foreigner. Part of this adjustment is in the language used.

Curiously, the police contact with Beverly Monroe comes closer to conversational style than in any of the other cases described here, largely because Detective Riley posed as Monroe's friend and ally throughout his conversations. This was the cover for his effort to persuade her, almost hypnotically, into believing that she was actually at the death scene of her lover. But the questioning of Pamela Gardner by the D.C. detectives most clearly illustrates how a successful conversational style can be managed in a police interview. They inquire without challenging, draw out facts without pumping, probe without cross-examining, and guide without dominating. Gardner soon self-generated her own slips, offering inconsistency after inconsistency, setting the stage for her ultimate admissions. The point here is that Detectives Corboy and Whalen, by being conversational rather than interrogational, by defusing their own asymmetrical power, and by being patient, encouraged Gardner to talk as she might in everyday circumstances, rather than as a trapped and defensive suspect at the police station. Through this openness, Gardner accomplished her own entrapment, self-generated her own guilt, and constructed the prosecution's case against her. The detectives patiently and courteously let her do the work that many other detectives try to do all by themselves. Rather than go after the suspect, Corboy and Whalen let the suspect come to them. Rather that insist that Gardner adopt to their construction of reality, they let her construct her own, knowing full well that their patience would be rewarded.

▶ Ask Clear and Explicit Questions

In addition to tape-recording all interrogation and confession events, law enforcement can protect itself from accusations of impropriety by developing an ability to ask clear and explicit questions. Infelicitous questioning techniques, as the Jerue case points out, invite multiple interpretations by the respondent. It is clear that people should be responsible for crimes they have committed, but not for crimes they have not done. If an ambiguous or unclear question has been asked, the defense has every motivation to point this out in court, often to the embarrassment of the government. Equally problematic are instances in which the vague question yields an equally vague answer for which the investigator (and, ultimately, the prosecutor) must infer the meaning. Inferential meaning, whether made by the subject or the prosecution, should be avoided at all costs in police investigations. The criminal case of John Z. DeLorean stands as a classic example of how the government lost its case because of false inferences from tape-recorded conversations (Shuy, 1993). The case of Shiv Panini, described in Chapter 8, provides similar examples of how the investigators inferred meaning far beyond that which was justifiable.

The ability to ask questions clearly and fairly is not easy to develop. The literature on interrogation techniques tends to focus on broad principles and categories, including advice to avoid making promises and threats but permission to flatter, talk roughly, trick, accuse, and even lie. Such broad principles are permissible and are not the subject of our attention here. Such manuals overlook, however, such things as *how* to be explicit rather than ambiguous (as in the Jerue case), *how* to clarify an ambiguous response by a subject, *how* to avoid intimidating a suspect (as in the Hill case), and *how* to avoid interrupting the suspect during a potentially exculpatory statement (as in the Monroe case). Such interrogation failures will surely call forth vigorous objection by alert defense attorneys, as well as careful analysis by linguists who assist them. One might argue that, in everyday life, ambiguity, intimidation, and interruption are common. Although this is true, it must be pointed out that the law enforcement interview/interrogation is not like "everyday life." The stakes are higher. Every word counts here, unlike most conversations, in which, even though one does not really understand, one can keep listening in the hope that comprehension will eventually be accomplished. There is no room for inferencing in the law enforcement interrogation. Things have to be clear and unambiguous. If they are not, it is law enforcement's job to request clarification until they are clear and unambiguous.

It has been noted repeatedly that the best evidence is self-generated and that the open-ended question is the obvious stimulus for such self-generation. "Tell me all about what happened yesterday," though it does not end with a question mark, actually functions as a question in that it is usually answered as though it were a formal question. Authorities on police interrogation place high value on beginning the questioning period with open-ended questions and then moving to *wh-* questions (who, what, where, when, how) for more specifics. This procedure is, in fact, how Detectives Corboy and Whalen sequenced their questions in the Pamela Gardner case described in Chapter 10. Police interrogation in most of the other interrogations in cases described here contain few if any open-ended questions. Instead, they abound with yes-no and tag question types.

▶ **Do Not Mix Interview Types**

On the basis of what can be gleaned from the authorities on the questioning practices used by law enforcement officers, the appropriate starting point with suspects is the *information interview.* Classic examples of ineffective interviews are common in the investigations of child sexual abuse, wherein child protection team interviewers, usually trained as social workers, unconsciously mix the information interview, required by law enforcement, with the *therapy interview,* which is intended to help the alleged victim, rather than to find out the facts in the case (Shuy, 1993). A close relative of the therapy interview is the *persuasion interview,* in which the interviewer attempts to persuade the subject that certain information is true even though the subject is resistant to that idea. The Beverly Monroe case is a persuasion interview, relatively untainted with the type of information for which the police interview was designed. The detective goes so far as to actually script what Monroe is allegedly saying and thinking in an effort to persuade her to his position. The interviews with Tamesia Russell in the DeWayne Hill case were persuasive by Russell's own admission. The evidence in the Goltz case shows that the government agent manipulated his subjects to say what he wanted them to say, playing on their guilt about procedural errors to escalate what they did into an alleged intentional felony. He scripted the written confession of the witnesses as well. In a sense, the interrogation, with its goal of eliciting a confession, is an exercise in persuasion.

► Look for Inconsistencies Before Trying to Determine Deception

The questioning of Shiv Panini, based entirely on the Reid instrument, sought very little information and was geared to determining only whether the suspect was being deceptive. A strong case must be made that investigators should begin the questioning of suspects with an information interview and continue to gather facts until such time as the suspect's fact reporting becomes inconsistent. At such a point, it is proper to move into a genuine interrogation in which the goal is to elicit a confession, but without scripting. In all the cases described in this book, with the exception of Pamela Gardner's questioning by Detectives Corboy and Whalen of the D.C. Police Department and, to a lesser extent, some of the interviews of Steve Allen, the interrogation style dominated.

One possible exception to this principle can be found in the technique of Sapir's (1987) SCAN procedure, wherein the use of written statements before any interviewing takes place can narrow down a suspect list. But even then, SCAN proves only that subjects *may be* deceptive, not that they actually are. Further interrogation must point out inconsistencies that offer the proof required. Currently available research on deceptive language offers little hope for deception detection, as Miller and Stiff (1993) so effectively argue.

► Tape-Record All Contacts

The National Institute of Justice recently commissioned a nationwide study of the use of videotape by law enforcement agencies. Study investigators concluded that, in 1990, about one third of all U.S. police and sheriff departments serving 50,000 or more citizens are videotaping at least some interrogations, primarily in homicide, rape, battery, robbery, and drunk driving cases (Geller, 1992).

Those departments that reported they videotaped interrogations said they initiated the practice to avoid defense attorneys' challenges, to help reduce doubts about the voluntary nature of confessions, and to help detectives' memory when testifying. The survey found that 97% of all departments that have ever videotaped suspects' statements continue to find videotaping useful. Every taping agency surveyed responded that it would videotape again. Most agencies experienced resistance from detectives when the practice was instituted, but after a few years of videotaping, disapproval by investigators fell to 26%. Interviews at agencies suggested that initial resistance was actually resistance to change in procedures of *any* kind, and not to videotaping specifically.

Of the case studies described in this book, only four settings used videotapes: the District of Columbia, Anchorage, Warren (Ohio), and Dallas. In two settings, no tapes of any kind were produced: Maryland and Montana (but bear in mind that the place names Maryland and Montana were changed for the purpose of anonymity of the subjects). In Bartlesville, San Diego, Baton Rouge, Monroe (Louisiana), and Powhattan County (Virginia), audiotapes were used. In all fairness, it must be noted that some of these cases took place over a decade ago, when video technology was not as accessible as it is today. It is clear from Geller's survey (1992) that the practice of videotaping suspects' statements is increasing.

Geller's survey also addresses the question of whether to tape the entire station house statement or only selected portions. The cost of taping and producing transcripts is often used to justify taping only partially. Defense attorneys who were interviewed clearly favored taping the entire statement, rather than recapitulations or selected parts of the interrogation. Detectives who tape entire statements expressed the belief that those who rely on recapitulations risk omitting potentially valuable words that a suspect may speak spontaneously but refuse to repeat on tape.

Perhaps the most significant finding in Geller's survey is that the majority of agencies surveyed opine that the videotaping experience has led to improvements in their interrogation techniques, including the use of old tapes as training materials for inexperienced officers. Another important finding is that because of videotaping, fewer allegations of coercion or intimidation were made by defense attorneys.

Videotaping suspects' statements would have most certainly proved beneficial to the defense in many of the cases described in this book, especially the cases of Steve Allen, Judge Goltz, Michael Carter, Beverly Monroe, and Shiv Panini. The best example of effective use of videotaping by the prosecution was clearly the Pamela Gardner case in Washington, D.C.

But even when tape recording is practiced by law enforcement, certain problems remain. For example, there is the matter of lost tapes (as in the Allen case), improper recording care (as in the nearly inaudible tapes in the Monroe case), and the malfunctioning recorder (common in criminal cases). Unless all of the interview and interrogation is recorded, the defense has good reason to ask why not, opening the prosecution to potentially embarrassing accusations of incompetence or bias. Even tape storage, copying, marking, and cataloging must be meticulously planned and carried out. Seemingly minor issues such as recording on both sides of an audiotape can escalate into larger problems at trial, especially when either defense or prosecution is desperately searching for a portion of a tape while the court waits for them to find the right side.

In recent years, I have noticed a growing acceptance of the need for linguistic assistance by prosecutors, law enforcement agencies, as well as defense attorneys. On several occasions, I have been asked by the Department of Justice and the FBI to help them with cases involving tape-recorded evidence, including cases involving federal judges accused of crimes. Perhaps even more notable, I have provided training to undercover DEA agents in language issues of drug transactions and, more generally, to the Organized Crime Task Force. One way to provide training in how to carry out a successful prosecution based on undercover, tape-recorded conversations is to play portions of the tapes of cases on which I have worked on behalf of the defendant, demonstrating the points that the defense will attack. Agents and I together then consider how the undercover officers might have said things in a better way to achieve their goals. One can learn as much from one's failures as from one's successes, as virtually any thriving businessperson or politician knows. Although all such linguistic training to date has concerned so-called sting operations, there is no reason why similar training could not be based on police interrogations and confession statements.

Law enforcement is a field that consists of many more components than law itself, although law is, of course, quite central. It is finally becoming evident that so-called specializations like, for example, law and medicine can no longer ignore the fact that to achieve the ultimate goals of justice and health, practitioners must develop their abilities in language interaction. Some 20 years ago, an article in the *New England Journal of Medicine* claimed that 95% of success of treatment depends on obtaining accurate information from the patient. It has taken two decades for the profession to reach the understanding that such accuracy is achieved through effective communication practices. Law enforcement is at this same turning point, if the cases represented here are any indication. Although matters of health are central to human existence, matters of justice are equally salient.

References

Andrews, P. P., & Peterson, M. B. (Eds.). (1990). *The analysis of tape-recorded conversations: Criminal intelligence analysis.* Loomis, CA: Palmer.

Aubry, A. S., & Caputo, R. R. (1980). *Criminal interrogation.* Springfield, IL: Charles C Thomas.

Azar, B. (1995, October). Police tactics may border on coercion. *APA Monitor, 28*(10), 27.

Bok, S. (1983). *Secrets: On the ethics of concealment and revelation.* New York: Pantheon.

Cody, M. J., Marston, P. J., & Foster, M. (1984). Deception: Paralinguistic and verbal leakage. In R. N. Bostrom (Ed.), *Communication yearbook* (Vol. 8, pp. 464-490). Beverly Hills, CA: Sage.

Donaghy, W. C. (1984). *The interview: Skills and applications.* Glenview, IL: Scott, Foresman.

Ekman, P. (1984). *Approaches to emotion.* Hillsdale, NJ: Lawrence Erlbaum.

Ekman, P. (1985). *Telling lies: Clues to deceit in the marketplace, politics, and marriage.* New York: Norton.

Foster, H. H. (1969). Confessions and the station house syndrome. *DePaul Law Review, 18,* 683-701.

Geller, W. A. (1992). *Police videotaping of suspect interrogations and confessions.* Wilmette, IL: Police Executive Research Forum.

Godfrey, E. D., & Harris, D. R. (1971). *Basic elements of intelligence: A manual of theory, structure, and procedures for use by law enforcement agencies against organized crime.* Washington, DC: U.S. Department of Justice, Law Enforcement Assistance Administration, Office of Criminal Justice Assistance, Technical Assistance Division.

Grano, J. D. (1993). *Confessions, truth, and the law.* Ann Arbor: University of Michigan Press.

Grice, H. P. (1975). Logic and conversation. In P. Cole & J. Morgan (Eds.), *Syntax and semantics* (Vol. 3, pp. 41-58). San Diego: Academic Press.

Gudjonsson, G. H., & Clark, N. K. (1986). Suggestibility in police interrogation: A social psychological model. *Social Behavior, 1,* 83-104.

Harris, D. R. (1976). *Basic elements of intelligence* (Rev. ed.). Washington, DC: U.S. Department of Justice, Law Enforcement Assistance Administration.

Hollien, H. (1990). *The acoustics of crime: The new science of forensic phonetics.* New York: Plenum.

Inbau, F. E., Reid, J. E., & Buckley, J. P. (1986). *Criminal interrogation and confessions.* Baltimore: Williams & Wilkins.

Johnson, M. K., & Raye, C. L. (1981). Reality monitoring. *Psychological Bulletin, 88,* 67-85.

Kamisar, Y. (1980). *Police interrogation and confession.* Ann Arbor: University of Michigan Press.

Kassin, S. M., & Sukel, H. (1997). Coerced confessions and the jury: An experimental test of the "harmless error" rule. *Law and Human Behavior, 21*(1), 27-47.

Leippe, M. R., Manion, A. P., & Romandzyk, A. (1992). Eyewitness persuasion: How and how well do fact finders judge the accuracy of adults' and children's memory reports? *Journal of Personality and Social Psychology, 63,* 181-197.

MacDonald, J. M., & Michaud, D. L. (1992). *The confession: Interrogation and criminal profiles for police officers.* Denver: Apache.

Marten, F. T. (1990). The intelligence function. In P. P. Andrews, Jr., & M. B. Peterson (Eds.), *Criminal intelligence analysis* Loomis, CA: Palmer.

McCormick, C. T. (1972). *Handbook of the law of evidence* (2nd ed.). St. Paul, MN: West.

McMenamin, G. R. (1993). *Forensic stylistics.* Amsterdam: Elsevier.

Miller, G. R., & Stiff, J. B. (1993). *Deceptive communication.* Newbury Park, CA: Sage.

Nissman, D., Hagen, E., & Brooks, P. R. (1985). *Law of confessions.* Deerfield, IL: Clark, Boardman, & Callaghan.

O'Hara, C. E., & O'Hara, G. L. (1988). *Fundamentals of criminal investigation* (5th ed.). Springfield, IL: Charles C Thomas.

Osgood, C. E. (1960). Some effects of motivation on style of encoding. In T. Sebeok (Ed.), *Style in language* (pp. 293-306). Cambridge: MIT Press.

Porter, S., & Yuille, J. C. (1996). The language of deceit: An investigation of the verbal clues to deception in the interrogation context. *Law and Human Behavior, 20*(4), 443-457.

Rabon, D. (1994). *Investigating discourse analysis.* Durham, NC: Carolina Academic Press.

Robinson, W. P. (1996). *Deceit, delusion, and detection.* Thousand Oaks, CA: Sage.

Royal, R. F., & Schutt, S. R. (1976). *The gentle art of interviewing and interrogation: A professional manual and guide.* Upper Saddle River, NJ: Prentice Hall.

Sapir, A. (1987). *The LSI course on scientific content analysis (SCAN).* Phoenix, AZ: Laboratory for Scientific Interrogation.

Searle, J. (1969). *Speech acts: An essay in the philosophy of language.* London: Cambridge University Press.

Shuy, R. W. (1988). Discourse-level language functions: Complaining. In J. Staton et al., *Dialogue journal communication.* Norwood, NJ: Ablex.

Shuy, R. W. (1993). *Language crimes: The use and abuse of language evidence in the courtroom.* Cambridge, MA: Blackwell.

Steller, M., & Koehnken, G. (1989). Criteria-based statement analysis. In D. C. Raskin (Ed.), *Psychological methods in criminal investigation and evidence* (pp. 217-245). New York: Springer.

Undeutsch, U. (1982). Statement reality analysis. In A. Trankell (Ed.), *Reconstructing the past: The role of psychologists in criminal trials* (pp. 27-56). Deventer, The Netherlands: Kluwer.

Wigmore, J. H. (1970). *Evidence in trials at common law* (Vol. 3). Boston: Little, Brown.

Woods, R. S. M. (1990). *Police interrogation.* Toronto: Carswell.

Wrightsman, L. S., & Kassin, S. M. (1993). *Confessions in the courtroom.* Newbury Park, CA: Sage.

Yeschke, C. L. (1987). *Interviewing: An introduction to interrogation.* Springfield, IL: Charles C Thomas.

Yuille, J. C., Hunter, R., Joffe, R., & Zaparniuk, J. (1993). Interviewing children in sexual abuse cases. In G. S. Goodman & B. L. Bottoms (Eds.), *Child witnesses, child victims: Understanding and improving children's testimony* (pp. 95-115). New York: Guilford.

Index

About
the Author

Roger W. Shuy is Distinguished Research Professor of Linguistics at Georgetown University, Washington, D.C., where he has taught graduate students for the past 30 years. He has specialized in issues relating language to the field of law for over two decades. He has testified as an expert witness in 45 criminal and civil cases throughout the United States and has served as linguistics consultant to defense attorneys, the U.S. Department of Justice, the Federal Bureau of Investigation, the U.S. Congress, and the Royal Canadian Mounted Police on hundreds of occasions. His book *Language Crimes* was published in 1993. He has also published many books and articles on the application of linguistics to the fields of education, medical communication, sociolinguistics, and language attitudes. He is Past President of the American Association of Applied Linguistics and currently serves on the editorial boards of the journals *Discourse Processes, Discourse and Society, International Journal of the Sociology of Language, Forensic Linguistics,* and *Hispanic Linguistics.* He is writing a book on bureaucratic language.

LaVergne, TN USA
20 July 2010
190089LV00002B/5/A